TRANSFORM YOUR LIFE WITH ALCHEMY

TRANSFORM YOUR LIFE WITH
ALCHEMY

A Practical Guide to Dissolve Self-Doubt, Balance Your Mind, and Center Yourself

KAREN FRAZIER

ROCKRIDGE PRESS

Interior and Cover Designer: Karmen Lizzul
Art Producer: Samantha Ulban
Editor: Jesse Aylen
Production Editor: Ashley Polikoff

All illustrations used license Shutterstock and The Noun Project. Author photo courtesy of Tristan David Luciotti.

ISBN: Print 978-1-64876-646-6 | eBook 978-1-64876-148-5
R0

For Jim

Contents

viii **INTRODUCTION:**
Greeting Your Inner Alchemist

1 **PART ONE:** UNDERSTANDING ALCHEMY

3 **Chapter 1:** The Root of Alchemy Is Change
and Transformation

15 **PART TWO:** THE BLACK PHASE

17 **Chapter 2:** Sparking Your Inner Fire
(Stage 1: Calcination)

31 **Chapter 3:** Washing Away Your Doubts
(Stage 2: Dissolution)

43 **PART THREE:** THE WHITE PHASE

45 **Chapter 4:** Sifting Makes You Stronger
(Stage 3: Separation)

57 **Chapter 5:** Letting Your Dark Meet Your Light
(Stage 4: Conjunction)

71   PART FOUR: THE RED PHASE

73   Chapter 6: Meeting Your Meditative Self Anew
(Stage 5: Fermentation)

85   Chapter 7: Awakening Your Enlightened Self
(Stage 6: Distillation)

99   Chapter 8: Becoming Your Centered Self
(Stage 7: Coagulation)

111   CONCLUSION:
Keep Doing Your Own Great Work

113   GLOSSARY

115   RESOURCES

116   REFERENCES

117   INDEX

Introduction

Greeting Your Inner Alchemist

Personal transformation is possible if you truly desire it. I believe readiness is the most important first step in metamorphosis. Once you set the intention for change, you're halfway there. After that, you need the right tools and processes to facilitate evolution. You've already taken the most important step: by choosing to read this book, you've indicated your intention and readiness to find a new, more authentic, empowered version of yourself.

In my work as an energy healer, metaphysician, alchemist, psychic medium, and life coach, I regularly assist with others' personal metamorphoses as they use powerful tools, such as meditation and visualization, to bring about lasting, meaningful change. It's a privilege to watch people who've stepped on the path of personal transformation as they experience evolution through the almost-magical process of self-realization and growth.

I transformed my own life using modern alchemical and metaphysical practices. About 20 years ago, I was in a bad marriage, my finances were a mess, and my health was poor. I hated my job and I was creatively unfulfilled and unhappy. I decided to change and found tools for personal transformation, such as meditation, visualization, and reframing. I've used these tools for more than two decades, and today my life is nothing like it used to be. I have meaningful and satisfying work and happy and supportive relationships. My health has improved and I'm prosperous and creatively fulfilled.

But make no mistake: Personal transformation doesn't happen on its own. It requires a combination of intention, willingness to put in the work, and the proper tools to support change. Alchemy is one system that offers these tools, and it's available to anyone who truly wants to evolve. Whether you wish to change one aspect of your life or to completely transform it, learning and using these tools will support you along your journey.

You've probably heard of alchemy in terms of the physical process of turning lead into gold, but you can also use it mentally, spiritually, and emotionally to bring about meaningful change. Through personal alchemy, you can shift your emotions and beliefs or create a new way to perceive and experience the world.

This book provides you with a set of tools for personal transformation using practices that follow the seven stages of alchemy, which we will explore in more detail in the first chapter. Each stage provides a map for personal transformation, and it all starts exactly where you are right now. The sequential processes are logical and easy to follow, and the ultimate result is finding your centered self—a more polished, purified, and authentic version of you, in body, mind, and spirit. Or, to put it into alchemical terms, your *golden self*.

Likewise, you'll work with the *four classical elements*—the elements that make up all matter: earth, air, fire, and water—as you move through each of the seven stages. By transforming these elements through the individual healing practices taught in this book in order to bring balance, you can create powerful and lasting personal change.

What's required of you is to do the work and maintain honesty and integrity throughout. Personal transformation requires self-awareness and the willingness to look deeply into your shadows to shine the light that's necessary for change.

Transformation is an ongoing process. Nobody has everything dialed in 100 percent of the time, so there's always something new to discover, tweak, or change. It's my experience that growth comes in fits and starts, sometimes slipping backward, sometimes getting stuck, and sometimes moving forward rapidly and joyfully. All of these forms are natural and normal, and I encourage you to honor your own process and treat yourself with kindness as you seek growth.

I'll be with you as you move through your transformation, offering tips and insights from my own experiences as well as from my "healing partners" (the phrase I use for clients because they are active in the process of their own change) to help you gain insight into your own metamorphosis.

I'm excited for you, and I'm humbled that you have chosen me to walk beside you on this journey. Meeting your own inner alchemist is empowering. Your life is about to change. Let's get started on your process of illumination and transformation.

PART ONE

Understanding Alchemy

Personal alchemy follows the seven basic stages used in the alchemical process: calcination, dissolution, separation, conjunction, fermentation, distillation, and coagulation. Here, I'll explain what each of these is to prepare you for your journey. I'll also introduce you to some of the tools and concepts you'll be working with, and I'll explain briefly how each can facilitate your own process. With this background in place, you'll be ready to begin working through the steps of personal alchemy to create lasting growth and change in your life.

CHAPTER 1

The Root of Alchemy Is Change and Transformation

During our first meeting many healing partners say, "I want to change, but I don't know how." What I hear in that statement is "I have the desire, but I don't have the tools." *Alchemy* is a set of concepts and processes that gives you those tools to bring about the growth and transformation you want in your life. In this chapter, we'll look at how alchemy, including the seven stages and the four classical elements, creates the foundation for true and lasting metamorphosis.

How Alchemy Began

Alchemy, or the art of transformation, is a precursor to chemistry. It started as a pursuit to better understand the universe through the transformation of a base metal (such as lead) into its most perfect form (gold). Today, alchemy is about creating physical, emotional, mental, and spiritual metamorphosis. It exists to turn something, or someone, into a better version of itself.

At its core, alchemy is a process of purification. In ancient times, this was most commonly described as turning lead into gold. Today it refers to the gradual process that brings about mental, emotional, and/or spiritual transformation, using its tools as a road map.

The use of alchemy for personal transformation requires deep, honest inner work, the desire for change, and the willingness to do the work. With roots in astrology, mysticism, psychology, and the classical Greek philosophy of the natural elements, alchemy is about discovering the imbalances in your own life and transforming them to create universal and individual balance. This is the work of being human: we come as spirits inhabiting imperfect bodies and minds, seeking to create universal balance through personal transformation.

Modern alchemy is practical. Use it to change your habits, attitudes, or experiences; the applications are endless once you understand its basic principles and practices. In this book, we'll focus on making changes that can shift how you experience and perceive your life—so you can live with more balance, peace, and joy.

Alchemy is also ongoing. There's always something new to discover about yourself, and there's always room to grow and change. You can use the seven stages of transformation over and over again to bring about large and small shifts, helping you live your best, most authentic, and most empowered life. Let's begin by exploring the seven stages of alchemical transformation.

The Seven Stages

The seven stages of alchemical transformation build upon one another. Each stage must be completed before moving to the next one. Each facilitates personal growth. Together the stages create a journey toward individual metamorphosis.

In the chapters that follow, we'll explore how each stage brings about shifts in body, mind, and spirit, contributing to how you live in the world at large. Before we get to the actual work, however, let's talk about the basics.

Calcination

Calcination, or "sparking the fire," as I refer to it in this work, is the first stage of the alchemical process. In chemistry, calcination refers to burning a substance until it becomes ash. In the art of personal transformation, calcination means taking the ideas, beliefs, projections, and filters through which you view the world and figuratively burning them so you can begin the process of change. Often, calcination begins almost accidentally, when something happens that makes you reevaluate some aspect of your life or self. However, you can also cause calcination through personal inquiry or a conscious decision to change.

Ego is the set of thoughts and beliefs you hold about yourself, as well as the filters through which you perceive the world. Your ego can control you, or you can control it. To some extent, ego creates a false sense of self shaped by a lifetime of experiences, conditioning, relationships, and beliefs. Ego is responsible for the sense of "I" that you have; it allows you to see yourself as separate from others. When the ego identifies with a false sense of self and is in control, it causes suffering. However, when you control your ego, it becomes a tool for living as your most authentic self.

Calcination is the first step in allowing your ego to work for you instead of the other way around. During calcination, you—or some force outside of yourself—spark the fire, turning that false self to ash so you can rise as a phoenix with a new sense of identity and purpose. Sparking the fire brings to light negative or incorrect projections caused by the ego. It deconstructs the pieces of your false self, creating space for a truer, healthier identity.

Dissolution

Dissolution, referred to in this book as "being honest with yourself," is the second phase of the alchemical process. In chemistry, dissolution involves dissolving or breaking apart a substance, typically by mixing or melting it into a fluid. In personal transformation, dissolution lets you take the self you deconstructed during calcination and join it with the energy of love and self-honesty so that you can put it back together in a new way.

Dissolution is a process that requires deep inquiry and personal honesty. You examine your beliefs and determine whether they support who you choose to be or whether a belief, habit, or relationship needs to be replaced with something new. Although you don't use a literal fluid for this process, the figurative fluid you use is the energy that underpins the entire universe: love. During dissolution, you blend love, truth, and light with the "ashes" of your former ego-driven self in order to grow. Please understand that it can be uncomfortable, but it's necessary for transcendent change.

Separation

In chemistry, *separation* allows you to convert a solution into individual, different products. For the purposes of this book, separation means being your authentic self—not just privately but also publicly.

Many of us present ourselves to the world with various masks in order to feel accepted, whether we're at work, play, or otherwise. We do it to ease the cognitive dissonance that can arise when our projections of self, others, and the world around us don't match our experiences. When we identify deeply with our ego we often falsely identify with these masks, because we lack crucial understanding of what is and isn't true about ourselves.

During separation, you take an honest look and figure out which aspects of yourself serve you and which don't. This is where you discover what's true about you and what isn't, which helps you cast aside false projections and live more authentically.

Separation allows you to determine who you are (and who you aren't). Think of it as sorting through the closet of your psyche and separating your various traits, beliefs, and projections into "keep" and "discard" boxes. During separation, your true identity begins to peek through, showing you who you can be moving forward.

Conjunction

In chemistry, *conjunction* refers to joining separate substances into something new. In transformational alchemy, I'll refer to conjunction as "getting to know your shadows." Every person has a shadow self. It consists of all the bits and parts of you that you're not fond of, so you separate them from your conscious self and lock them away in the dark.

When a soul enters a human body, we travel from Oneness and unity with Source into a world of *duality* and separation. We go from being One with all to identifying ourselves as separate from everything around us. Although this sense of separation is an essential part of the human experience, part of the work of being human is to remember (or rejoin with) the Oneness by recognizing that we share common energy with everyone and everything. Hiding our shadows from ourselves and others keeps us separate and alone, preventing us from moving back toward the Oneness of Source. It's this movement toward Oneness that allows us to become our purest and highest version of self.

In duality, all human traits exist on a scale anchored by polar opposites. Each trait can have either a positive or a negative expression, or a more neutral expression that exists somewhere between the two poles. For example, with the personality trait of courage, one pole is cowardice and the other is bravery. In various circumstances, all of us respond somewhere along the spectrum between the two.

When you feel good about where on the spectrum your experience falls, you integrate it into your conscious ego and use it to boost your self-identity. When you feel poorly about it, you relegate it to your subconscious (or *shadows*), where you can ignore it and forget it ever happened. This sorting of experiences into conscious and subconscious creates a lack of balance that results in personal consequences such as guilt, shame, distrust, projection, lack of self-esteem, acting out negatively, and inauthenticity.

In conjunction, however, you work at reintegrating your shadows into the whole. It's necessary and important work to achieve the harmony you're looking for. Acknowledging, examining, and reintegrating your shadows helps you step away from the fear of exposure (both to self and to others), which is essential to living more authentically, lovingly, and joyfully.

Fermentation

In chemistry, *fermentation* occurs through a chemical breakdown of various substances when other microorganisms are introduced. The result is something new, like fermenting a grain mash with yeast to produce alcohol. In personal fermentation, you take the raw materials you have created from the first four stages and form a fresh, new sense of self. In this book, I refer to this stage as "meeting your meditative self."

During fermentation, you create a new, more authentic self by combining what remains of your old self with your highest consciousness, or your soul. The magic ingredient for fermentation is meditation, which lets you connect with your ancient Source energy to expand your consciousness and grow into the highest and truest version of you. It's the process by which your consciousness expands toward enlightenment.

Distillation

In chemistry, *distillation* is a process of purification. In the liquor-making process, fermented alcohol is boiled during distillation to remove impurities. In the art of personal transformation, I refer to this step of the alchemical process as "celebrating your conscious self." During distillation, you take part in self-purification to move toward Source energy and your Divine self.

Coagulation

In chemistry, *coagulation* occurs when particles join together to create something larger. In the work of personal metamorphosis, I call this "creating your centered self." This is where you emerge as a higher version of yourself with a new sense of wholeness, balance, and completion. In coagulation, you can recognize and live from a place of "we" rather than "I" because you are less ego-involved and more connected with the world around you.

The Great Work

The ultimate goal of alchemy is something called *the Great Work* or *Magnum Opus*. In traditional alchemy, this involved working with the *prima materia* (prime material, such as lead) and using alchemical stages to produce the *philosopher's stone*, which was the theoretical substance required to turn lead into gold. For the purposes of personal metamorphosis, the Great Work is you; it is the greatest achievement of transformation as you move from your old self toward the highest, greatest, and most golden version of yourself that you can be.

The Essential Elements

Alchemy also uses the four classical elements of earth, air, fire, and water. Just as energy is divided into opposite poles, it's also separated into these four distinct forces of nature. You'll find this elemental division of energy in various cultural, healing, and divination traditions, such as astrology, polarity therapy, and (with slightly different names) Eastern traditions like feng shui and martial arts.

The Greek philosopher Empedocles first described the four classical elements in around the fifth century BCE. These elements were believed to explain the four fundamental natures of matter that made up the entire physical universe. Each element has properties that directly affect the human body, mind, spirit, and emotions. Imbalances in these elements can cause a number of issues.

In alchemy, elemental balance is essential for personal transformation. We'll work with each element both literally and metaphorically as we move through the alchemical phases.

 ## Earth

Earth energy is heavy, dry, and dense. It's grounded energy that helps connect the individual to the physical plane. It gives stability, security, consistency, and persistence. An overabundance of earth energy creates stubbornness, sluggishness, laziness, repression, and inflexibility. A lack of earth energy causes flightiness, unreliability, over-idealism, and fickleness. Earth balances air.

 ## Air

Air energy is light and fast moving. It's the energy of the spiritual, as well as of intellect and reason. It brings flexibility, curiosity, and openness. Too much air may result in unrealistic idealism, deceitfulness, or the inability to focus and bring creative ideas to fruition. Too little air can cause sluggishness, inflexibility, or laziness. Air balances earth.

Fire

Fire energy is active, aggressive, fast moving, and engaged. It represents drive and ambition. It confers passion, enthusiasm, and confidence. Too much fire may cause irritability, obsession, or arrogance. Too little may result in lack of drive and passion or a poor sense of self. Fire balances water.

▽ Water

Water energy is fluid, flowing, and flexible. It can adapt to anything that surrounds it, or, in motion, it can actively shape what it flows through. Energetically, water represents emotion and compassion. An excess of water energy may result in being oversensitive, easily hurt, and moody. An underabundance may make you restless or impatient, judgmental, or ego-driven. Water balances fire.

The Ways You Will Grow

Using alchemy for personal transformation is about growth. The exercises in this book, which we'll explore together shortly, are designed to bring shifts in body, mind, and spirit. Everyone is a combination of body, mind, and spirit, and attention to each is essential for metamorphosis.

Growing Your Mind

Alchemical transformation frees your mind from programming created by social, familial, and religious expectations. The alchemical mind is flexible, growth-oriented, and open to shift. It means being willing to take a deeper look at thoughts and beliefs to determine if they really serve you. Having an alchemical mind lets you dismiss preconceived notions, break outdated attachments, and release patterns that no longer serve your greatest good.

Growing Your Spirit

Having an alchemical spirit frees you to dwell as an individual soul with consciousness of the Oneness from which you came, of which you are still a part, and to which you will return. The alchemical spirit is open to guidance from higher beings, such as angels and spirit guides, and is in constant communication with your higher self. The alchemical spirit intuitively recognizes various forms of spiritual guidance and how each supports the growth of your soul in the journey of life.

Growing Your Body

Having an alchemical body means discovering and engaging in nutrition, movement, and environmental practices that honor the container your spirit has chosen to travel in and the physical universe in which you dwell. When you live in an alchemical body, you exist harmoniously with your own body and with the physical universe. It's a process of cooperating with the various environments that support you, including your home and work lives, your communities, the world, and the universe.

Bringing Your Alchemical Self into the World

Your ultimate goal is to bring your transformed self into the world so you can be more authentic in all aspects of your life—including your interactions with the people, places, and situations around you. It's a way of living consciously, both within your own body, mind, and spirit and within the greater context of the world. It allows you to be your most centered self—the highest version of you—in all you think, say, and do. It also motivates you and provides the tools that stimulate shifts as you recognize new changes you wish to make.

The Tools You Will Use

Throughout each stage, I'll provide a number of tools to help in your transformation. Each tool serves to polish your golden self and facilitate the process of metamorphosis.

Meditations

Meditation is a transformative practice requiring presence and awareness. Meditation practices, such as noticing your breathing or engaging in focused movement, help you focus on the present.

Mantras

Mantras are contemplative statements that focus awareness. They may be powerful "I am" statements (*affirmations*), or they might be more esoterically focused on a concept you wish to cultivate.

Visualizations

Visualizations let you imagine the change you wish to experience. They are guided meditations that use visual imagery to help you envision living as your highest self. During these meditations, you will visualize what you want to experience in order to live a more fulfilled life. Visualizations are usually 5 to 10 minutes long and are easily adapted to your own desires and choices.

Chakra Work

Chakras are energy centers that connect your physical body (body and mind) to your etheric body (emotions and spirits). You have seven chakras, one that corresponds to each stage of alchemical transformation. You can use various forms of chakra work to focus on and balance each specific energy center.

Journaling Prompts

Journaling is one of the best ways to process information. Journal prompts offer ideas on which to reflect as you transform. The prompts invite you to examine unconscious beliefs and integrate them into your life in new ways. Even if you're not a writer, don't worry. You can journal as feels best and most natural for you, whether that means video journaling, or audio journaling, or any other way of recording your impressions and feelings that works for you.

How to Use This Book

There's no one-and-done content in this book. Rather, it provides a road map to return to anytime you recognize something you wish to transform. You can use the process to make small changes or to completely overhaul your life. Because the stages are progressive, if you feel stuck or frustrated, you can return to a previous stage and rework it, and you can always move forward at your own pace. It's up to you how you engage in the alchemical process, but simply by holding this book in your hand you have indicated your willingness to grow. Congratulations! You're now ready to begin your own process of alchemical personal transformation and empowerment.

FINDING INSPIRATION AND SURPASSING YOUR ROADBLOCKS

Typically, the path of metamorphosis is not a straight line. You might surge ahead, creep forward, move backward, pause, explore a detour, stumble, or get stuck. All are normal parts of the process. There's no "correct" transformational journey, so it's essential to honor your own process with compassion and kindness.

I find many of my healing partners beat themselves up if they aren't continuously moving forward at a set pace. However, it's important to recognize that the path you take is always the right one for you in that moment. Detours, backtracking, and slowdowns are not only allowed but encouraged. When I notice a healing partner feeling frustrated with their progress, I remind them that no one's journey, no matter how far they've wandered, is without its gifts, and I encourage them to allow and accept the process with self-compassion.

In the spirit of self-compassion and encouragement, I've included extra inspiration for when you're feeling discouraged, hesitant, or doubtful. Throughout this book you'll find sidebars that share others' progress as a source of encouragement, to help you move forward on your own path and overcome negativity, frustration, or self-doubt. As you read their stories, recognize that your path is uniquely your own and that no matter what arises, you can't do it wrong as long as you have the sincere intention for change.

PART TWO

The Black Phase

(Calcination and Dissolution)

The *Black Phase*, also called *Nigredo* or "blackness," is the first, most intense phase of alchemical transformation. Rooted in decomposition, decay, and burning, the Black Phase breaks down your old self to kick-start metamorphosis. Although it may seem dark or distasteful, before you can build something new it's necessary to illuminate and remove attachments, beliefs, and patterns that keep you from reaching your full potential. Think of the Black Phase as making room for change by getting rid of the things that no longer serve you. In the chapters that follow, we'll delve into the Black Phase stages so you can emerge with greater purpose and clarity.

CHAPTER 2

Sparking Your Inner Fire

(STAGE 1: CALCINATION)

Calcination is a process that sometimes begins spontaneously, though it can also be intentional. In this chapter, we will explore how to identify the change you want to experience and ignite the process, providing you with calcination ideas and exercises as you begin your journey of transformation. Calcination is one of the most thoughtful and intensive phases of alchemical metamorphosis, but it's also necessary to begin the work of growth and change.

Calcination Basics

When you're in the calcination phase, there are several elements you can work with. The corresponding chakra, classical element, colors, crystals, and oils are all tools that can assist during the calcination phase, allowing you some freedom to customize your own work as you see fit.

Associations with calcination include:

» Purpose: destruction of the ego

» Chakra: root

» Colors: black or red

» Element: fire

» Crystals and stones: black tourmaline, hematite, garnet, spinel, shungite, onyx

» Essential oils: cinnamon, patchouli

How to Spark Your Fire

Calcination is the process of breaking down things that no longer serve you in order to create the space for transformation. Before the fire is sparked, you may have ego attachments, conditioned behaviors, and subconscious beliefs that keep you trapped in a persona that no longer serves your greatest good.

What sparks the fire may be either intentional or unintentional. For example, in my life, an external source (the death of my father) sparked one of my most significant processes of change. At other times, I have intentionally sought out change because I realized I was unhappy or unfulfilled in some way.

Often the igniting incident for alchemical transformation arises out of something that shocks your system, as my father's death did for me. It may be an event of major significance, or it may be something small that triggers dissatisfaction, igniting the desire to change.

Recognizing Igniting Incidents

I often tell my healing partners that negative or painful emotions such as discomfort, pain, sadness, anxiety, or depression are an indication that it's time to make changes in your life. In fact, recognizing whether you are ready for calcination or an igniting incident is as simple as this: If you feel bad, then something needs to change. If you feel good, then chances are that change isn't necessary at the moment. Some incidents or feelings that might ignite the calcination phase and spark your inner fire include things like:

- the end of a relationship
- illness or injury
- depression
- grief
- job loss
- a general sense of dissatisfaction
- boredom or ennui
- anxiety
- lack of motivation
- general malaise
- fear
- loss of interest in certain activities that once brought you pleasure
- feeling trapped
- helplessness
- frustration

Using the Igniting Incident as Impetus for Change

Once you recognize that you are experiencing an igniting incident, you have the option to enter a transformative process. In some cases, you do this without a thought because you are so shaken up by the igniting experience that not metamorphosizing is unthinkable. In other cases, however, artifacts of ego may hold you back and make you hesitant or unwilling to change. It is in these cases, when calcination isn't naturally ignited, that you need to set your ego aside and set the conscious intention for change through alchemical transformation.

Ego's Role in Calcination

Have you ever stopped to think about what makes you different from everyone and everything else around you? After all, your essence is energy—the same material (in different forms) as all that exists in the physical universe as a part of your embodied experience. I call this Source energy, which is our true essence. It is what we are before we are transformed through birth, what we are while we experience life in a physical body, and what we will return to after we leave the earthly plane through the transformation of death.

All incarnated souls leave the Oneness of Source and enter into human bodies in order to discover the dualities that exist in the embodied experience. Even as newborn babies, human souls have something more than bones and skin that separates self from other and allows them to experience themselves as an individual: ego. It is ego's purpose to create a sense of "I" or "me" so that each soul can fully experience being in a body, separated from Source energy.

Ego starts as a way to identify the "I" that is inherent in being an individual. In this way, it is a healthy tool to help us recognize the difference between me and you or this and that. Ego allows us to label all things that arise within our human experience so that we can fully immerse ourselves in the process.

Throughout our lifetime, ego continues to build as we catalog and label our experiences; reactions; emotions; social, family, and religious conditioning; and all the other aspects of a human life. It is the container that holds our energy essence so we can have the experience of self and other. As embodied souls, we process everything through our egos, which are like eyeglasses we put on that allow us to see the world in our own unique way.

Humans, however, tend to be overly ego-identified. We become so wrapped up in our egos that we use them as our primary form of self-identification, forgetting or ignoring that there is so much more to us than the *small "I"* that ego allows us to experience. So although we need ego in order to identify as an individual, we also allow it to control us in ways that keep us from realizing our full potential.

Ego is actually a highly fragile construct, but it is fiercely protective of the small "I" to the point that it separates our self from the Oneness. Because ego fights so hard to protect the small "I," it deploys a host of defensive strategies that keep us bound by fear, in pain or discomfort, and blocked from becoming our golden selves. An uncontrolled ego will obfuscate, project, judge, criticize, and externalize in order to protect the fragile sense of self it creates. These actions of ego keep you from metamorphosis.

Therefore, one of the key processes of calcination is the destruction of the unhealthy, controlling aspects of ego. This lets you voluntarily transform into someone who uses ego as a tool for self-realization instead of allowing ego to control you and block your growth.

The experience of ego is always bookended by two key transformations. In the human life cycle, every embodied soul experiences the transformations of birth (leaving the Oneness to enter into the small "I") and death (release from ego to return to Source). Other transformations, like growing, maturing, aging, getting sick, and getting well, are likewise a normal part of being alive and happen without much effort on your part. Some transformations, however, such as the metamorphosis of personal growth, are optional. They require the destruction or lessening of ego through calcination in order to move you into the highest version of yourself.

Recognizing Ego's Defense Mechanisms

In calcination, you'll likely uncover defense mechanisms the ego uses to reduce anxiety and protect identity. Here are some common defense mechanisms you might uncover as you spark the fire for change:

» Displacement: taking out your doubts, frustrations, and anxieties on someone else

» Repression/suppression: forcing unwanted memories into your shadows

» Projection: attributing your undesirable qualities to another person

» Avoidance: not dealing with unpleasant tasks or feelings

» Dissociation: removing yourself from your experience

» Rationalization: explaining away unacceptable behaviors

Sparking the Fire in Body, Mind, and Spirit

As a human, you are more than just the collection of tissue, space, and fluid that makes up your body. You are also a thinking, feeling being with a mind, and the energetic essence that is spirit. In order to be a wholly integrated being, you cannot separate body, mind, and spirit, as each aspect of yourself acts upon the others. When you transform one of these aspects of self, you must transform the others as well.

During calcination, when you spark the fire in one of these aspects of self, it ignites the flame in each of the others, too. So, to complete your transformative process, you have to look equally at all aspects of yourself to assess patterns of thoughts, words, triggers, habits, feelings, and actions that don't serve your highest good.

Let's look at a few examples of how you might spark calcination in body, mind, and spirit.

Body

Illness, injury, and dissatisfaction with your physical form can all ignite the fire for transformation in your body. For example, having a heart attack at a young age might drive you to make physical and emotional changes to improve your health. Likewise, dissatisfaction with your current weight or activity levels might ignite you to eat better or move more.

Mind

A number of things might spark the fire of calcination in your mind; for example, recognizing patterns of thought that don't serve you, discovering you are harshly critical and overly judgmental toward yourself and others, or the desire to rid yourself of unproductive habits. When you recognize these thought patterns, you can choose to transform them through the alchemical process and bring about mental, emotional, spiritual, and physical changes.

Spirit

Spiritual igniting events that spark calcination might include things such as an existential crisis, a loss or reimagining of your current belief system, or a dark night of the soul. For example, I previously mentioned my father's death as something that ignited spiritual calcination for me. When my dad died, I realized that many things I'd spent years worrying about, like gaining his approval, were merely wasted time. This allowed me to make spiritual changes in my relationships with a number of people in my life, including my mom. I realized I'd always held back in my relationship with her because I felt I needed to present to her the me she wanted or expected me to be. My dad's death showed me how I'd denied both of us an authentic relationship because of my desire for parental approval, and it felt like a wasted opportunity. This realization helped me transform my relationship with my mom into a more honest and authentic one.

Life Changes from Calcination

Although calcination is just the first step in alchemical transformation, it is the most important and intense one, because it puts you on the path to metamorphosis. You're breaking down patterns of behavior, belief, and thought that no longer serve you. Although this can feel like an existential crisis, it also creates space to welcome change in your life. When you burn something down, you're left with endless room to build something newer and better than you ever could have imagined.

CALCINATION EXERCISE #1: **MEDITATION**

Crystal Fire Meditation

YOU WILL NEED:

- » **table or desk**
- » **candle**
- » **matches or lighter**
- » **large, transparent red crystal, such as hematoid quartz**
- » **chair**
- » **journal and pen (optional)**

➤ In a darkened room where you won't be disturbed, place a candle in a candleholder on a table or desk and light the candle with a match. Place the crystal in front of the candle so you can see the light shining through it. Sit comfortably in a chair near the table and gaze at the crystal.

➤ Focus on the candlelight shining through the crystal, taking deep breaths in through your nose and out through your mouth until you are in a relaxed and meditative state.

➤ Ask yourself the following questions, allowing the answers to arise without trying to control them:

- » How do I feel physically?
- » What is my current emotional state?
- » How connected do I feel to spirit?
- » What physical practices and habits make me unhappy?
- » What thoughts make me unhappy or uncomfortable?
- » What spiritual practices do I need in my life?
- » What makes me unhappy or dissatisfied?
- » What makes me uncomfortable?
- » Which relationships don't bring me joy? What about them is unsatisfactory?

➤ Take the time to meditate on the answers as they arise. Don't feel the need to do anything other than recognize and acknowledge that these are flash points in your life that can spark the desire for change. Sit with your answers and, if you feel so inclined, write them in your journal.

Meeting the World with Your Fiery Self

Once you've ignited the fire for transformation within you, start observing the world around you. Notice when you engage in thoughts, words, and behaviors that you've identified as being the source of unhappiness. When you catch yourself in these behaviors, replace them with something that supports your highest vision of self. For example, if you catch yourself thinking negatively about something, replace it with a positive thought instead.

This process may leave you feeling uncertain about who you are versus who you want to be, but that's to be expected. Rejoice in the fact that you are no longer weighed down by these things and remind yourself that you are in the process of transformation. Letting go of that which no longer serves you has put you on the path to metamorphosis.

If someone in your life expects you to continue your negative patterns, such as a sibling who has placed you into a box since childhood, kindly and compassionately let them know that you've decided to let that aspect of yourself go so you can grow and change. If it is someone close to you, you may even wish to ask them to help and support you on your journey.

When he was young, Mark's mild autism made him feel so awkward that he developed coping mechanisms to appear "normal." He emulated others' behaviors while suppressing emotions he thought made him seem vulnerable. Mark's ego became wrapped up in appearing neurotypical.

Because he only understood the neurotypical experience through observation, Mark developed incorrect assumptions about neurotypical people. Based on these, he grew angry, judgmental, resentful, and stressed.

The American Heart Association names stress as a significant contributor to heart disease, so it's no surprise that, with as much rage and stress as he suppressed, Mark had his first heart attack in his early fifties. This experience of physical illness shocked Mark so much that it became the igniting event for his process of personal transformation.

He began to challenge his assumptions, learned to express his emotions instead of suppressing them, and developed a number of spiritual and energetic practices, including visualization and energy work, to help him change his thoughts, behaviors, and beliefs. Today, he's more relaxed and in control of his emotions, and he continues to work on improving his physical and mental health. As a result, he is much happier and more content with life. Although Mark's transformation remains ongoing, he is putting in the work to emerge as his own centered and golden self.

Root Chakra Awakening

YOU WILL NEED:

» **cinnamon-scented incense or candle, or cinnamon essential oil and diffuser**

» **incense holder and matches (if using incense) or a candleholder and matches (if using a candle)**

» **timer**

➤ In a darkened room where you won't be disturbed, light the incense or candle and place it in the holder or add the essential oil to the diffuser and turn it on. Set the timer for 15 minutes. Sit comfortably on the floor or on a cushion and close your eyes. Breathe in the aroma, focusing on pulling the scent in through your nose and blowing it out through your mouth until you are in a meditative state.

➤ Visualize your root chakra at the base of your spine as a rotating wheel of red light. Each time you breathe in the aroma, visualize it being pulled in through your nose, traveling down your spine, and joining with the rotating red light of your root chakra. As the aroma blends with the light in the chakra, visualize the wheel growing to fill your whole bottom, hips, legs, feet, and lower abdomen with the red light and aroma of the cinnamon.

➤ During the meditation, allow any thoughts that arise to drift into your awareness before you release them and return your attention to your root chakra. Continue until your timer goes off, then gradually return to awareness.

It's natural to resist the ignition of calcification. The destruction of self, even the false self, can be uncomfortable or even feel like an existential crisis. It's essential that you work on observing yourself without judgment as you work through calcination. Journaling can be helpful during this process.

You can use anything as a journal—a notebook, a blank book with a pretty cover, a piece of paper, or even a blank document on your computer. In your journal, complete the following sentences.

1. The negative pattern I have identified is . . .
2. This negative pattern affects my life by . . .
3. It makes me think . . .
4. It makes me say . . .
5. It makes me do . . .
6. It makes me believe . . .
7. The most important reason I want to release or change this pattern is . . .
8. Without this negative pattern in my life:

   - I will feel . . .
   - I will experience . . .
   - My relationships will . . .
   - My health will . . .
   - My job will . . .
   - I will do . . .
   - I won't do . . .
   - I won't be . . .
   - I will be . . .
   - I can . . .

9. Changing this pattern will allow me to . . .
10. I look forward to . . .

What Comes Next?

Identifying your flash points for change is a necessary first step in the process of transformation. Once you've identified those and decided you're ready for change, you are ready to move on to the process of dissolution. However, if you're not sure that you've identified what you want to change or if you feel you haven't examined the issue enough to ignite the fire for transformation, reread the chapter and return to the exercises. Remember, change is ongoing—you can use this process over and over again, either for simple changes or total metamorphoses, as you continue to identify what's keeping you from being the highest version of yourself.

CHAPTER 3

Washing Away Your Doubts

(STAGE 2: DISSOLUTION)

Whereas calcination can begin spontaneously, dissolution is a more deliberate act involving deep self-honesty. Once you've identified the patterns that no longer serve you and sparked the fire for personal transformation, it's time to delve into your psyche through awareness practices. In this chapter, we'll explore how bringing awareness into your alchemical transformation can help wash away any doubts about metamorphosis. We'll also talk about using tools of contemplation to continue shifts in body, mind, and spirit.

Dissolution Basics

When you're in the dissolution phase, there are several tools you can work with to assist in the process. You can work with the corresponding chakra, colors, classical element, crystals, and oils in your own ways and use them in the exercises that follow.

Associations with dissolution include:

» Purpose: self-honesty, contemplation, going with the flow

» Chakra: sacral

» Colors: orange, rust, brown

» Element: water

» Crystals and stones: smoky quartz, orange calcite, carnelian, peach moonstone

» Essential oils: orange, neroli, bergamot

How to Be Honest with Yourself

Dissolution is a time to take a deep and honest dive into self-awareness. During calcination, you took the first step: identifying patterns that didn't serve you. As you move into dissolution, you'll look deeper into yourself to move further past the ego's defenses. This self-loving act can help refine your intention for change and wash away any lingering doubts about whether you really do want transformation.

Recognizing Denial, Avoidance, Regression, and Doubt

The ego's first line of defense in protecting the small "I" includes things such as projection, perception, conditioning, false beliefs, filters, masks, bad habits, and negative patterns. In calcination, you identified protective ego patterns and ignited the fire of desire to change them through personal metamorphosis.

However, that's only the first step. Your ego will go to great lengths to protect the small "I" that forms your conditioned identity, especially when ego suspects it is under siege. While calcination started to strip away layers of conditioning, ego keeps additional weapons in its arsenal as a secondary line of defense to protect its fragile sense of self.

Four of ego's main defense mechanisms in this phase are denial, avoidance, regression, and doubt. These natural psychological tendencies are pure ego projections. Ego uses them to protect the small "I" so you can hold on to your false sense of self. However, when you hold on to an ego-driven identity that is untrue, it prevents you from becoming your golden self. Therefore, you must overcome denial, avoidance, regression, and doubt. These unhealthy coping mechanisms are most likely to arise after calcination, but they can also come up any time throughout the process of personal transformation.

To transform, you have to first recognize when denial, avoidance, regression, and doubt appear and then acknowledge they are projections of ego. It's essential to understand each in turn so you can identify it when it occurs.

DENIAL

According to the Mayo Clinic, *denial* is a coping mechanism that ego uses to protect you psychologically by giving time to process something distressing. It is perhaps most commonly recognized as the first phase of grief that Dr. Elisabeth Kübler-Ross proposed in her 1969 work, *On Death and Dying*.

Being in denial is refusing to acknowledge or accept a truth as a means of self-protection. It's a coping mechanism, but an unhealthy one that can have negative psychological, emotional, spiritual, and physical consequences.

For example, when one of my healing partners who is a nurse noticed her daughter was having symptoms consistent with type 1 diabetes (juvenile diabetes), she spent several months in denial that her daughter might have this illness, even though her medical mind knew differently. It took her about six months of active denial before she was able to process emotionally what she recognized intellectually and have her daughter tested and treated for her condition.

Though denial is a primary stage of grief, you can be in denial about virtually anything that causes you distress or pain, generates anxiety, or makes you feel conflicted, out of control, or vulnerable. For example, you might be in denial about difficulty in your romantic partnership, an illness, or a less-than-desirable personality trait.

AVOIDANCE

In *Psychology Today*, author and psychologist Dr. Alice Boyes named avoidance as another ego-driven coping strategy, similar to denial. Whereas denial is the refusal to acknowledge unpleasant things, *avoidance* occurs when you go out of your way to avoid things that make you feel psychologically uncomfortable.

For example, refusing to pay a large and unexpected bill or set up a payment plan with the collections company is an example of an avoidant behavior. Avoiding certain activities or situations to reduce your anxiety would be another example. Likewise, your ego uses people-pleasing as an avoidant behavior to try to control how someone else feels about you.

REGRESSION

A 2014 article in *Psychology Today* discussed *regression* as a coping strategy in which individuals return to earlier patterns of thought, feeling, or behavior. Neurologist Sigmund Freud was the first to identify regression as a negative coping strategy, suggesting it was a return to childish behaviors. That is certainly one aspect of regression, but you don't have to act like a child to regress.

Here's an illustrative example of regression from my own personal experience: I've always felt like somewhat of a misfit in my family, which led to a lot of self-esteem issues. Growing up in my very boisterous family, I was an often quiet, anxious wallflower. In college, I was able to move out of my shyness and social anxiety, becoming outgoing and outwardly confident. However, on school holidays when I returned home, I returned to my anxious, self-contained persona instead of manifesting the self I was when I was at school. I regressed as a coping mechanism to get me through family holidays.

DOUBT

Doubt, as a coping mechanism, is the ego's attempt to control anxiety by generating feelings of uncertainty or lack of conviction. Doubt is insidious. It often first appears as a whisper-quiet voice in the back of your mind, where you barely notice it. However, as ego perceives a growing threat, it stops whispering its doubts and starts shouting them.

Doubt has many disguises, so it's important that you recognize them. Doubt almost always lies; doubts are made-up concerns that are more unlikely than likely to come true. Some forms of doubt include:

- » inability to decide
- » worry or anxiety about the future
- » rehashing the past
- » feeling overwhelmed
- » fearing something won't work
- » worrying about the consequences if it does work
- » feeling uncertain
- » feeling unconfident
- » believing you're not up to the task
- » thinking "I'm not good enough" or "I'm not enough"
- » second-guessing yourself
- » heeding your inner critic
- » believing "I can't"
- » thinking "I should" or "I shouldn't"
- » feeling like an impostor

Overcoming Ego's Defense Mechanisms

Dissolution's purpose is to help you recognize, acknowledge, and overcome the defense mechanisms ego uses to keep you in the small "I." In dissolution, you practice deep self-honesty during contemplation to overcome these hurdles to personal transformation. Moving forward, we'll look at some available tools so you can leap over the hurdles instead of tripping on them.

Embracing Your Honest Body, Mind, and Spirit

At first, the defense mechanisms ego uses to keep us in the small "I" seem real and insurmountable. The work of dissolution is to recognize these coping mechanisms for the untruths that they are. This requires self-honesty, personal integrity, self-love, and the willingness to recognize, acknowledge, and overcome your own nonsense.

Honest Contemplation Is Key

There is not a person walking the planet who isn't embroiled in their own nonsense, because ego is so good at creating it. The difference between an alchemist in the process of personal transformation and the average person, however, is an ongoing unwillingness to accept these thoughts and beliefs as personal truth. You'll be able to do this when you can do the hard work—honestly and nonjudgmentally exploring your mental, physical, and spiritual patterns, projections, beliefs, triggers, and habits. It starts with recognition, which often comes in a flash that we ignore. When this recognition comes, instead of ignoring it, spend some time in meditative practices or with thoughtful journaling to explore what the issue is and how it affects your life.

Nonjudgment Is Essential

One of the more difficult aspects of honest contemplation is our tendency to criticize ourselves. It's human nature upon recognizing a pattern, thought, or behavior that doesn't serve you to engage in some self-blame, name calling, or harsh self-judgment. (For example, "How did I never see this about myself before? I'm such an idiot!") However, personal transformation is not the place for judging yourself, as self-criticism pushes you away from enlightenment rather than driving you toward it.

Make your best effort to observe without judgment. Pay attention and notice when you start to judge yourself. When you do, step back, take a deep breath, and remind yourself that you have always done the best you can with where you were in your life and the tools you had available. When you know differently, you *do* differently. When you have more effective tools, you *use* more effective tools. You can't change the past, but you can focus on the now and make your best effort to move forward in a positive way.

Talk to yourself as you would to a friend. What would you tell a loved one who was judging themself harshly? You'd probably say, "You did your best in the given circumstances. Look at how many wonderful, positive qualities you have and focus on those." Tell yourself these things, too.

Practice Unconditional Self-Love

Personal metamorphosis through alchemy is a practice of self-love. You transform and change not because you don't love yourself, but because you do. You deserve to present in the world at all times as the highest version of yourself in each moment. Working to achieve that ideal is an act of unconditional love.

Lasting and meaningful change can only come from self-love, even though it may be sparked by things you discover about yourself that you don't like. Without the love of self as a motivation, you will, at some point, abandon the process. It's why, when you've attempted to change for another person, it's never really stuck. The true driver of personal transformation is individual desire, and that desire only comes when we recognize that we owe it to ourselves to become a higher version of self.

Have you ever set off on a weight loss journey or a fitness kick to please another person? How did that go for you? Most people find that when they set out to lose weight or change their appearance because another person wants them to, it seldom sticks. However, when the impetus for weight loss or improved fitness is your own sense of self-worth, the change is more likely to become permanent. Thus, the "right reason" to personally transform isn't because someone else wants you to; it's because you love yourself enough to desire better, no matter what form that betterment takes.

DISSOLUTION EXERCISE #1: **MEDITATION**

Water Scrying

YOU WILL NEED:

- » **chair**
- » **table**
- » **large bowl filled with water**
- » **three drops**
  orange or bergamot essential oil
- » **candle and matches or a Himalayan salt lamp**
- » **journal and pen**

➤ Sit comfortably with a table in front of you in a darkened room where you won't be disturbed. Place a bowl of water on the table and add the essential oil. Place the lit candle or Himalayan salt lamp behind the bowl of water (the bowl will be between you and the light source).

➤ Gaze at the water's surface, taking deep breaths of the essential oil aroma in through your nose and out through your mouth until you reach a relaxed and meditative state. Bring to mind one of the issues you uncovered during calcination. Lean over the bowl and speak the issue aloud into the water.

➤ Continuing to gaze at the water's surface, unfocus your eyes and notice any images or thoughts that arise. As you receive them, breathe them in through your nose and visualize them traveling down your spine and into your sacral chakra, which is a rotating orange-colored wheel of light just below and behind your belly button. Then breathe the message back out through your mouth and clear your mind, focusing on the water once again. Do this for as long as you feel comfortable (10 to 15 minutes is adequate).

➤ When you are done, write any insights you gained in your journal.

Meeting the World with Your Honest Self

Stepping into the world more honestly can make you feel vulnerable. However, in cultivating more self-honesty, you not only transform yourself but also transform how you present in the world. A more truthful you engages more honestly in relationships as well. And this increased self-honesty can strengthen some relationships while causing others to fall by the wayside. Know, however, that if a relationship dissolves because you are presenting more authentically within it, then it is not one that will serve the truest version of yourself. Step away with love and gratitude, knowing that by ending a relationship that no longer serves you, you are energetically making room for more that do.

Things that no longer serve you often fall by the wayside during alchemical transformation, and this is perhaps most true during dissolution. This can feel stressful and cause sadness, but it is the natural progression of growth; things that don't serve you must fall away to make room for new and greater things. Allow yourself to grieve any losses you experience, and when you are ready, open your arms and embrace the space the losses have created to welcome in bigger, brighter, and better things.

FINDING INSPIRATION

Before I found my more fulfilling path, I worked as a marketing communications writer for an industrial automation company, and I disliked how my supervisor treated women. I stayed because it paid well and I could work from home most days because I lived so far from the company.

I began engaging in personal inquiry through journaling about my unhappiness with work. It required contemplation and deep self-honesty, and I felt the shifts starting to happen. As I shifted and changed, I grew even more dissatisfied with my job, but I just couldn't bring myself to break free from it.

One day at work I noticed my supervisor mistreating someone, and I spoke up because I just couldn't take it anymore. It was not well-received. About two weeks later, my supervisor suddenly demanded I come to the office every day or be laid off. I lived two hours away, so I was laid off.

I was in a panic, but there was also part of me that recognized this as my chance to create the career I desired rather than accepting the one I had. I think you know the rest: today, I work from home as a full-time writer, editor, life coach, energy healer, teacher, and psychic medium. I love my work. It is meaningful and creatively fulfilling. However, without self-honesty, I might still be working in a job where I was comfortable but unhappy.

Cleansing Waterfall

YOU WILL NEED:

» **running water sound generator (such as a phone app)**

» **timer**

» **journal and pen**

➤ In a darkened room where you won't be disturbed, turn on the sound generator and sit or lie comfortably. Set the timer for 15 minutes. Close your eyes and breathe deeply, in through your nose and out through your mouth, making sure you pull your breath all the way into your belly and release it fully before taking the next.

➤ When you reach a relaxed and meditative state, imagine you are walking along a peaceful, wooded path in autumn. The leaves are turning orange, and the wind gently rustles through them. Notice the sound of running water off in the distance and walk toward it.

➤ In front of you is a beautiful waterfall cascading down a hillside filled with brilliant fall foliage in all colors. Approach the waterfall and lie down underneath it so the water streams over you and into you. As you lie under the water, notice any thoughts or images that arise. Breathe them in and then release them on the next breath, returning your attention to the sensation of the water as it pours over you.

➤ When your timer goes off, return to your body. Express gratitude for the experience and take a moment to write your impressions in your journal.

Let's do some writing to help you overcome doubt, denial, avoidance, and regression. In your journal, complete the following sentences.

1. Something I'd like to change about myself is . . .
2. What's keeping me from making this change is . . .
3. Continuing with this makes me feel I am . . .
4. The belief that keeps me locked in this behavior is . . .
5. When I ignore this behavior, I feel . . .
6. When I avoid looking at my own role in this, I notice . . .
7. When I deny this is a problem, I notice . . .
8. When I make progress but then return to this issue, I feel . . .
9. I'm afraid that if I start to change, I will . . .
10. I'm afraid that if I don't change, I will . . .
11. My life after making this change will feel . . .
12. My relationships after making this change will be . . .
13. My work after making this change will be . . .

What Comes Next?

After completing dissolution, you may be feeling a little raw. It's a natural side effect of deep self-honesty; recognizing your own role in things can be difficult, but it's ultimately rewarding. If you still don't feel you've explored everything as honestly as you can, you can always reread the chapter and rework the exercises until you're ready to move on. During this time, be kind to yourself and engage in practices of self-compassion and self-love. In the next phase, you will begin to rebuild by taking what you have broken down and re-forming it into a more powerful and authentic version of you.

PART THREE

The White Phase

(Separation and Conjunction)

The *White Phase* of personal transformation is also called *Albedo*. You've experienced the decay and decomposition generated in the Black Phase; now comes the alchemical process of sorting and separating to return light to the spaces left behind by the darkness. In this phase, you will go through the next two stages of alchemical personal transformation: separation and conjunction. Here, you'll begin sifting through the patterns, attachments, and beliefs you discovered in the shadows and gently cleanse them to reveal their clarity.

CHAPTER 4

Sifting Makes You Stronger

(STAGE 3: SEPARATION)

We've reached the separation stage of alchemical transformation; it's time to engage in personal housecleaning. Just as when you clean out those messy closets, sorting through items you wish to keep and discard, in this chapter you'll take your own internal inventory to find what serves you and what doesn't. This phase allows you to discover which parts are compatible with your golden self and which no longer serve your greatest good. Separation introduces you to your true self.

Separation Basics

When you're in the separation phase, there are several tools, such as the corresponding chakra, crystals, and essential oils, that can assist you in the process.

Associations with separation include:

- » Purpose: finding your authentic self
- » Chakra: solar plexus
- » Colors: yellow, gold
- » Element: air

- » Crystals and stones: citrine, pyrite, yellow tiger's eye, amber, golden calcite
- » Essential oils: lemon, rosemary, juniper, chamomile

How to Be Authentic about Who You Are

Which parts of you are authentic and which are not? These can be difficult questions, and it's okay to grapple with them as long, or as often, as you need to. As you contemplate the answers to these questions, what comes to mind? Often, our own inauthenticity runs so deep and is so resistant to exposure that we are blind to it until we intentionally take a closer look. Through the mindful sifting process of separation, our inauthentic traits begin to fall by the wayside.

What is your *authentic self*? It's dwelling within the truth of who you are. Authenticity means recognizing your true self and sharing it with the world. It sounds simple, but most people have multiple aspects of themselves that are inauthentic.

Why People Are Inauthentic

So why would someone choose to be something other than who they are? Once again, the answer lies in ego and the enduring desire to be liked, admired, and accepted. Inauthenticity is a risk mitigation strategy, and it's almost always protective. If you don't share your authentic self and you fail, are rejected, or come up short in some other way, you can tell yourself that it doesn't matter because it wasn't your personal failing, but rather the failing of your *persona* that caused you to stumble.

According to *Encyclopaedia Britannica*, the psychologist Carl Jung coined the term *persona* to describe the personality people project to others instead of displaying their authentic self. Persona is a role we play, or a mask we wear, in order to fit into the various aspects of our lives. For example, a shy introvert who presents a jolly and boisterous personality when out in public with friends is presenting the persona of an outgoing extrovert. Likewise, someone who constantly suppresses their true feelings in order to stay in a relationship is presenting the persona of being agreeable and easy to get along with.

So what's wrong with that? Why shouldn't we try to fit in by putting on different masks? It can be a thorny question. At the heart of it, leading with your persona is about the need for control. By showing others the aspects of self you think they want to see, you are attempting to control their perception of you, and that requires a *ton* of energy that could be better placed elsewhere. When you try to control someone's impression of you, you're not just wasting time and energy; you're denying them the chance to meet your actual beautiful soul—and yourself the opportunity to get to know the real them as well.

When we are born, we are purely who we are, since, on some level, our awareness is still connected to Source energy. However, even as infants, we develop our persona as we interact with adults. As we discover which behaviors and traits they deem acceptable and which they don't, we adjust our personality accordingly. As we get older and our world expands, we refine our persona to fit in with others, like teachers, peers, spiritual associates, community, country, workplace, and the world at large. By the time we're adults, we've moved so far away from our authentic selves and into our personas, that we may have very little familiarity with—or appreciation for—our own truth.

That being said, as far as acceptance from others goes, having a persona can be pretty darn effective. The persona allows you to move seamlessly from one group or experience to another while feeling relatively secure, since what you present to the world brings you at least some level of acceptance from others. Dwelling within your persona feels safe, because if another person doesn't know the real you, then it won't hurt as much if they reject you.

Unfortunately, taking a deep dive into an inauthentic persona requires a lot of energy that could be otherwise focused on meeting your true potential. Likewise, not being your authentic self blocks your path to true joy, harmony, and balance in your life. It keeps you from developing true self-worth, self-love, and self-esteem, which pulls you further away from reconnecting your essence and Source energy. It also blocks the real connection that comes when one soul recognizes another as they walk the path of human incarnation. You cannot transform into your golden, centered self if you are inauthentic.

How to Recognize When You Aren't Being Authentic

So how can you tell when you're being inauthentic? When you've stuck to a persona or personas for much of your life, it may be hard to tell, but it's safe to assume that everyone with an ego (that is, everyone) has some level of inauthenticity in how they present themselves to others. Some signs you are being inauthentic include:

» Instead of speaking your truth, you go along.

» You compromise your principles to be liked.

» You're worried about what others think of you.

» You go out of your way to make others admire you.

» You suppress parts of your personality that you fear others won't like.

» You're afraid to say no.

» You have different personalities around different people.

» You engage in "code switching" and use different language or speech patterns around different groups of people.

» You ignore your intuition.

» Appearances are more important to you than substance.

» You're a perfectionist.

» You habitually engage in escapist behaviors such as drinking, overspending, gambling, etc.

» You make choices based on what will bring you power, money, or some other material gain.

» You're a conformist who follows the crowd.

» You judge others who fail to conform.

» You're willing to compromise your morals for others.

» You feel resentful.

» You avoid conflict.

» You feel defensive.

- » You are afraid to share your opinion.
- » You take everything personally.
- » You're unhappy.
- » You're afraid if people knew the real you, they wouldn't like you.
- » You tell lies, exaggerate, or make up stories.

If you see yourself in any of these behaviors, read on to discover how to find your unique sense of authenticity.

Finding Your Way to Authenticity

Separation allows you to find your way back to authenticity. It involves not only looking at your shadows but also welcoming them and allowing them to coexist with your public persona. It also involves allowing and expressing your true feelings, facing self-doubt and fear, and expressing who you truly are. As you engage in alchemical separation, you'll begin to find your way back to yourself so you can be your truest and most authentic self all the time.

Being Authentic in Your Body, Mind, and Spirit

Chances are your persona has invaded your collective body, mind, and spirit. During separation, you'll sift through each of these important aspects of self in order to find the gem underneath that is the real you. Once you've discovered that gem, you'll be able to inhabit your life in a new way that feels more natural and less stressful.

Body

Authenticity in body involves what you wear, how you groom yourself, what you eat, and how you move, among other physical aspects. A great modern-day example of physical authenticity versus inauthenticity is the social media phenomenon of the "selfie." Are all of your selfies carefully composed, taken from the perfect angle, and heavily filtered, or are you willing to share images in which you don't look quite so perfect?

In separation, you'll sift through the physical ways you present yourself to others. You'll determine whether these ways are meaningful to you or if you're doing them to influence how others think about you.

For example, I am a fifty-something-year-old woman whose hair is about 75 percent gray—at least, judging by my roots, I suspect it's somewhere around that amount. So I color my hair. During a pandemic shutdown when I wasn't able to get my hair colored, a lot of that gray grew back. It was the first time I'd seen it for ages. As my gray grew in, I had the time to think about whether I colored my hair because I liked it or if I was doing it to fool other people into thinking I was younger than I was. It seems silly, but it made me realize I color my hair because I like it colored. That realization has given me the freedom to play with other hair colors because they're fun, rather than staying within the narrow window of what's considered an acceptable hair color for a woman in her fifties.

Mind

Authenticity of mind includes things like sharing your true thoughts and feelings, being willing to say "I don't know" when someone asks you a question, and pursuing your true passions with gusto. For example, I know someone with an inauthentic mind who always has to appear to be the "smartest person in the room." It's so important to them that people think they're smart that if a topic comes up that they're not well-versed in (and nobody can know EVERYTHING), they'll change the subject and dominate the conversation with facts and figures. They were once in a class I was teaching about crystal healing, and several times throughout the class they interrupted me to start talking about their area of expertise, which wasted the time of others who had paid to take the class.

In separation, you'll sift through the emotional and mental components of your mind, asking yourself, "Is this true for me?" and "Does this matter to me?" to discover your most intellectually and emotionally honest self.

Spirit

Spiritual authenticity is all about walking your true path, regardless of what others think about it. For me, that was finally getting away from the corporate world, where I made a lot of money and got a ton of respect, and stepping instead into spiritual work as an energy healer, author, and psychic medium. Even though I had done the separation work and realized that was my true path, it still felt like a huge risk because there is so much societal (and, in my case, familial and religious) disapproval relating to some of the more "woo-woo" pursuits. However, embracing my true "woo" has been life-altering in the best possible ways. Sorting through your own spiritual truths can have the same effect on you.

SEPARATION EXERCISE #1: **MEDITATION**

I Am Breathwork

YOU WILL NEED:

» **journal and pen**

» **sheet of paper (optional)**

➤ On a blank page in your journal or sheet of paper, draw a vertical line down the center. At the top of the left column, write "I AM." On the top of the right column, write "I'M NOT." Then, write a list of 10 to 20 examples in each column. You can include traits you have, such as "I am passionate," "I am joyful," etc., and traits you don't have or don't want, such as "I am not self-involved" or "I am not clumsy."

➤ Sit comfortably with your lists in front of you in a place where you won't be disturbed. Place both hands over your solar plexus chakra, which sits at the bottom of your sternum. Close your eyes and breathe in through your nose and out through your mouth until you reach a relaxed and meditative state. Now open your eyes. As you inhale, in your mind (not aloud), read an I AM statement, pulling it inside of you and down into your solar plexus. Hold for a count of three.

➤ As you exhale, in your mind read an I'M NOT statement, visualizing it moving up from your solar plexus and out of your body on exhale. Hold for three seconds.

➤ Continue doing this for each I AM and I'M NOT statement. When you've finished the list, breathe in one final time, thinking, "I AM." Pull it into your solar plexus and hold for three seconds. With a final exhale, think "RELEASE," and on that breath, release all that you are not.

➤ Write any impressions in your journal.

Sharing Your Authentic Self

Although sharing your authentic self may feel risky, the more you do it, the more empowered you can become. Over time, being authentic takes less effort and feels more natural. Soon, you'll wonder why you ever thought you needed to put up a front at all.

With greater authenticity comes more freedom. By being authentic, you're letting go of all the energy you once used to keep your masks in place and sending it toward something more soul satisfying. Of course, being more authentic means that some of your less authentic activities and superficial relationships may end. If they do, take any time you need to grieve, knowing that releasing these attachments will make way for new, better things more aligned with your true self.

As someone who presents more authentically in the world, you'll attract more things that bring you pleasure, including relationships and friendships, practices, hobbies, and meaningful work—those things that most resonate with you. This will help you step into your centered and golden self.

FINDING INSPIRATION

Issa grew up with an abusive mother and learned to behave in certain ways to appease her. As an adult, Issa continued seeking her mother's approval with her appearance and her job, and by running errands and doing chores for her. At family gatherings, Issa cooked and cleaned instead of spending time with people, which she resented.

When Issa described the situation, I asked why she felt she needed to do that if she hated it. She replied that her family expected it; they'd think she was making drama if she stopped. I asked how she knew that was true and if she'd ever tried doing something differently. When I asked, a light came on. Issa didn't know if it was true, because she'd never tried anything else.

At Issa's next family gathering, she decided not to do those things and see what happened. The next time I saw her, she was a different person. Her hair and clothes were different, and she seemed lighter and happier. It turned out that when Issa discovered she could attend a family gathering as a guest instead of as a servant and everyone would still like her, she started to question the other behaviors she engaged in to earn her mom's approval. This realization was life changing. Issa began stepping into her authentic self more frequently and enjoying her life and family more.

Solar Plexus Activation

YOU WILL NEED:

» **matches**

» **sandalwood incense**

» **incense holder**

» **timer**

» **comfortable cushion or yoga mat**

» **citrine or pyrite crystal**

» **journal and pen**

➤ Find a quiet place where you won't be disturbed. Light the incense and place it in the holder. Set the timer for 15 to 20 minutes. Lie comfortably on a cushion or yoga mat and place the crystal on your solar plexus chakra, which sits at the bottom of your sternum. Place your hands over the crystal, resting them gently on the solar plexus.

➤ Close your eyes and breathe in through your nose and out through your mouth. As you breathe in, visualize your solar plexus chakra as a spinning wheel of golden light. Imagine that the air you are breathing is a glowing gold color. Breathe it in, drawing it into your solar plexus, and visualize it mingling with the wheel of light. Hold your breath for a slow count of three, feeling the warmth of your hands spreading the golden energy from your crystal into your solar plexus.

➤ Exhale, feeling the golden light from your solar plexus expanding upward on your breath and spreading throughout your entire body. Continue, breathing in and out, until your timer goes off.

➤ Write any impressions in your journal.

More than any other alchemical phase, separation is about self-definition, or deciding who you are. To keep this authentic, you must practice inquiry, especially if you're feeling stuck in this phase or aren't sure how to move forward in your process. You can use this journal prompt any time you are taking your own inventory and deciding what serves you and what doesn't. In your journal, complete the following questions:

1. The aspect of self I wish to inquire about is . . .
2. What I know about this aspect that is true is . . .
3. What I know about this aspect that is false is . . .
4. When I display this aspect, I feel . . .
5. If I no longer engaged in this aspect, I would feel . . .
6. If I no longer engaged in this aspect, I would be . . .
7. If I no longer engaged in this aspect, I would think . . .
8. If I no longer engaged in this aspect, I would know . . .
9. I can release this aspect because . . .
10. I cannot release this aspect because . . .
11. Moving forward, I will not . . .
12. Moving forward, I will . . .

What Comes Next?

Separation work lets you see yourself in entirely new ways, which can be freeing. As with the other stages, it's an ongoing process you'll return to over and over as you seek new self-definition and new ways to grow and change. If you need to inquire more deeply, reread the chapter and rework the exercises until you're satisfied. Then you can move onto the next phase of transformation, which is the work of conjunction.

CHAPTER 5

Letting Your Dark Meet Your Light

(STAGE 4: CONJUNCTION)

Everyone has a shadow self buried deep in their subconscious. A lot of people go through their entire life never confronting their shadows, which can unfortunately keep them from becoming fully integrated individuals. This self-imposed stoppage, in turn, blocks transformation and growth. In alchemical transformation, you purposefully step into the shadows of your subconscious in order to illuminate them and reintegrate them into the whole being that will become your centered and golden self.

Conjunction Basics

When you're in the conjunction phase, there are several tools you can work with. You can work with the corresponding chakra, crystals, element, or essential oils to customize the process.

Associations with conjunction include:

» Purpose: bringing light to your shadows

» Chakra: heart

» Colors: green, pink

» Element: earth

» Crystals and stones: rose quartz, moss agate, serpentine, morganite, mangano calcite, watermelon tourmaline

» Essential oils: rose, jasmine, pine

Learning to Share Space with Your Shadow

Picture yourself in a dark basement with no light at all. As your eyes adapt to the darkness, you can see differences in the density of the darkness that appear to be shadowy figures. Now imagine that, as you hear a shuffling sound, one of those shadows moves toward you. It's terrifying, because you have absolutely no idea what is there in the darkness. All you know is that it's moving in your direction. Suddenly, you remember you have a flashlight in your pocket, so you pull it out, turn it on, and shine it in the direction of the shadow. There you see your dog, smiling at you as it wags its tail. By shining a light on the shadows, what was once scary is now friendly, approachable, and even a welcome presence.

This is a metaphor for shadow work. Throughout our lives, we take aspects of ourselves that we dislike—or that we think others dislike—and shove them into the darkest corners of our subconscious, in the basements of our minds. There your characteristics sit, dismissed and forgotten, unless you bravely journey into the dark space and shine a bright light on all you have hidden there. Once you do, you discover that those phantoms lingering in the darkness of your subconscious aren't scary after all.

Conjunction allows you to intentionally explore your shadows. It's important that, as you do the work, you treat yourself with unconditional love and deep compassion. These are the two ingredients required to bring light to your shadows so you can be born anew.

How Your Shadows Came to Be

As social creatures, human beings crave love, companionship, and approval. We learn at a very young age which aspects of ourselves generate approval, make people "love" us, and attract others to us. In fact, from our first cry of hunger after we're born, we are conditioned to behave in ways others want us to and in ways that get others to do what we want. We also grow to believe that to be worthy of love we must conform to what others want from us. In the overhang of this belief, our shadows are born.

This type of conditioning is an ongoing process that occurs practically every waking moment of every day, although it's so subtle and ingrained in human interaction that we seldom recognize it's happening. And as we grow, the number of people in our lives participating in our conditioning multiplies exponentially; we have playdates, go to school, make friends, participate in community and religious activities, grow into adulthood, cultivate romantic partnerships, and get jobs.

Every time we do something that someone in one of our communities appears to disapprove of, we internalize that message. We then use it to decide which aspects of ourselves are acceptable and therefore safe to display and which are unacceptable and need to be hidden. The things we hide become our shadows. We don't see that the entirety of us is worthy of love, not just the shiny, conditioned parts we present to the world.

Humans also operate within a set of personal and societal values that we establish throughout our lives. Whereas some ethics are deeply personal views we come to on our own, even more of them come from others—people in our lives, media, politicians, educators, teachers, employers, and members of the clergy. By the time we reach adulthood, we're walking around with values that we believe are our own but that have actually originated from those we've encountered in the world around us.

Often, these human values don't align with our soul values, because human values tend to support the small "I," whereas soul values support universal love and Oneness. When our human self is out of alignment with our soul self, spirit sends us feedback in the form of discomfort, but we seldom recognize what it means or why we're experiencing it. Because we don't recognize the source of our discomfort, we ignore the voice of our higher self and continue with our human pursuits, nudging our shadow selves even deeper into our personal recesses.

Each time we ignore the messages from our higher self, it damages our small "I." We don't recognize where that discomfort is coming from or what its purpose is; we simply know we feel uncomfortable and like ourselves a little less. Yet instead of contemplating why we dislike ourselves, we sublimate the shame we feel and bury it deep in the shadows of our subconscious, where we hope it will never see the light of day again.

Returning Shadows to Light

Personal transformation requires that we shine a light on our shadows so we can see them more clearly. It also demands that we meet our shadows head-on so we can eventually reintegrate those forgotten, rejected aspects of ourselves back into our whole being. In that way, we can love ourselves as fully and unconditionally as we deserve to be loved. Fortunately, much like turning on the light in a dark basement, shining the light on your shadows makes them seem a lot less scary. Conjunction is the flashlight you use to reveal that what you thought would be frightening to see is actually quite benign.

Getting to Know the Shadows of Your Body, Mind, and Spirit

Like all of the other aspects of personal transformation, shadow work is ongoing; there are always new shadows to uncover and hidden parts of ourselves to expose to the light. In all of my years of shadow work, I find that I uncover new shadows when I'm ready to deal with them and not before, and I've never found a shadow that I wasn't willing or equipped to deal with. This is true of my healing partners as well. When you uncover a shadow, you'll have the tools needed to work with it and reintegrate it into your authentic self; don't worry that you'll uncover something you're not equipped to deal with. If you feel ill-equipped to work with these issues, you can always seek health through therapy, counseling, or medical assistance as needed. As you uncover each shadow, treat that shadow—and your entire self—as you would a small child or beloved pet you love unconditionally: gently, kindly, compassionately, and without judgment.

Let's take a look at some of the ways your shadows may manifest and how you might uncover them.

Body

This type of shadow is all about the physical. Physical shadows you may uncover include:

» body image issues, such as feeling too fat, too thin, or not strong enough, as though your unique body is somehow less than ideal

» shame associated with physical choices you've made, such as a pregnancy termination, drug or alcohol use, or similarly delicate situations

» shame associated with sexuality and sexual expression

» issues associated with gender identity and sexual orientation

» issues such as lack of care for the environment

» repressed acts of violence you've perpetrated or that have been perpetrated against you (abuse, assault, etc.)

» lack of personal care or poor health hygiene habits

To meet your physical shadows, it's important that you start to pay attention to your body. In my work as an energy healer, I've discovered that we can uncover most of our physical shadows by listening to what our physical symptoms try to tell us. Symptoms are your body's alarm system telling you something is out of balance. Therefore, in order to do body shadow work, I recommend the following:

1. Listen to your body; don't ignore physical pain or discomfort (even when it's minor). It's best to catch a symptom at its earliest stage, when it's the easiest to resolve.

2. When you do notice a physical symptom, close your eyes, focus on the symptom, and ask, "What are you trying to tell me?" Then listen for an answer.

3. When a shadow is revealed, refrain from judgment. Instead, express your gratitude for its revelation and wrap it in love.

Mind

Shadows from your mind include personality traits, thoughts, and judgments you aren't proud of. Shadows associated with the mind include:

» being harshly critical or judgmental of self or others

» being unkind and engaging in gossip

» negative self-talk

» general negativity

» mental health issues

» intellectual challenges

» acts of dishonesty, either personally directed or outwardly directed

» guilt and shame about things you've done

» internalized messages you've received from others

» labels you've applied to yourself and others or that others have applied to you

To find your mind shadows, notice when you feel a recurring or persistent sense of mental or emotional discomfort and go within. Try the following:

1. Go someplace safe, close your eyes, and breathe into the feeling.

2. Allow any emotions to arise without trying to block them.

3. Ask, "Why am I having this emotion?" Then listen and allow the answer to arise.

4. Refrain from judgment, give thanks for receiving the answer, and wrap the shadow you have revealed in love.

Spirit

Spiritual shadows arise when you are out of alignment with your soul's purpose. Your spiritual shadows might include:

» acting without integrity

» lacking compassion for self or others

» ignoring your inner voice in pursuit of ego gratification

» allowing yourself to be controlled by fear instead of love

» failing to engage in spiritual practices that nurture you

You can find spiritual shadows in much the same way as you find mental and emotional shadows. When you notice a sense of existential discomfort, it indicates you are out of alignment with your spiritual purpose and should go within. Spiritual shadows often arise in dreams. To find spiritual shadows, try the following:

1. Before you go to sleep, ask to be shown your shadows.

2. Pay attention to darkness in your dreams. This may include people with dark hair, dark eyes, and dark clothing, as well as dark rooms, dark objects, or even underground places such as caverns, caves, holes, or cellars.

3. When you wake, write down your dream and use a dream dictionary to interpret it.

CONJUNCTION EXERCISE #1: **RITUAL**

Nourishing Your Shadows with Earth

YOU WILL NEED:

» **small strips of paper and a pen**

» **terra-cotta flowerpot**

» **potting soil**

» **plant seedling of your choice**

» **small spade**

» **water and a watering can**

» **rose quartz**

» **journal**

➤ Identify two or three shadows using the process outlined earlier. Write each one on a small piece of paper. Hold each piece of paper to your heart and beam love from your heart into the words written there. As you do so, say aloud, "I bring my shadows into the light of love."

➤ Put the pieces of paper into the flowerpot and cover them with potting soil. As you cover them, say aloud, "As the earth nourishes my shadows, my shadows nourish the earth."

➤ Transplant the seedling into the dirt over the shadows, adding more soil as needed. As you plant, say, "My shadows nourish new growth."

➤ Finish by watering the plant and placing the rose quartz in the pot to symbolically send continued love to your shadows.

➤ Write any impressions in your journal.

Sharing Your Shadow Self

Meeting your own shadows may feel risky, but once you've exposed them to the light of self-awareness, it becomes easier to go out into the world and share your newly integrated shadow self with others. This doesn't mean you need to go out and tell everyone what you uncovered; sharing your shadows with others may make you feel uncomfortable or deeply vulnerable. However, you're more than welcome to share your shadows if you wish or if it helps keep you accountable.

How might this look? It may be as simple as recognizing that you're suppressing your shadows or noticing yourself responding in a conditioned way to something in order to gain approval. It might be something even more powerful, such as stepping into and expressing a new identity that you've reunited with and living with it proudly in the world.

I've done shadow work regularly for more than two decades, and I can tell you this: when I finally step into my shadows and meet the parts of me I've suppressed, it is incredibly freeing. The freedom in no longer hiding parts of self from you or others is life-altering and expansive. Likewise, once you stop spending energy hiding things from yourself and others, you have that much more energy to invest in things that bring you peace, love, and joy instead. As your shadows leave, they make space for anything you'd like to put in their place.

Mai was in an unhappy relationship. As she described it, she did and gave everything, and her partner only took, which she resented.

I asked when it had started, and Mai told me it had always been that way. I asked why, if her relationship started out that way, did she resent it, since that was the dynamic from the beginning.

"It's a pattern I have in all of my relationships," Mai told me. "I carry the weight, and everyone else just coasts."

"Why do you think that is?" I asked.

Mai told me she hated conflict, so she found it easier to just get along.

"What would happen if you didn't try to get along?" I asked.

"They'd think I was a bitch," was Mai's reply.

"Are you?"

This started Mai's shadow work, during which she recognized that she'd buried parts of herself to avoid appearing bitchy. Mai secretly believed that expressing personal desires made her unpleasant or difficult. However, when she looked at that shadow with self-love, Mai recognized that having wants and needs was a natural part of being human, and she was able to reintegrate that shadow back into her whole. This allowed Mai the freedom to build relationships in which she was willing to state her own needs, which ultimately led to more satisfying and equal relationships without resentment.

Earth-Shadow Heart Chakra Visualization

YOU WILL NEED:

» **chair**

» **timer**

» **journal and pen**

➤ Go somewhere you won't be disturbed and sit comfortably in a chair with your bare feet flat on the floor. Set a timer for 15 minutes. Place both hands over your heart and breathe in through your nose and out through your mouth until you reach a relaxed and meditative state.

➤ Visualize your shadows as literal dark shadows throughout your body and aura. Notice that your shadows first seem dense in appearance, but when you look closely into them, you see that they are actually just tiny particles of darkness surrounded by lots of space.

➤ As your hands warm your heart, imagine a green light flowing from your hands and into your heart chakra, which is a spinning wheel of green light in the center of your chest. See the green light grow, expanding to fill all the spaces between the particles of your shadows, surrounding them completely.

➤ Once the green light envelops your shadows, notice the light and shadows flowing downward through your spine and into your legs and feet, then into the earth, where your shadows are nourished.

➤ Continue to visualize the flow of green light and shadows until your timer goes off or until all of your shadows have flowed into the earth under your feet. When you're ready, open your eyes.

➤ Write any impressions in your journal.

Use this journal prompt to help you illuminate your shadows when you're feeling stuck and unable to move forward. If you're completely honest, the prompts can help uncover issues you've hidden even from yourself (the things we dislike about ourselves tend to be the ones we relegate to our shadows). Complete the following sentences:

1. I don't like _____ about myself.
2. I am afraid others won't like me if I . . .
3. I know others don't like me when I . . .
4. My worst trait is . . .
5. When I display this trait, I feel . . .
6. When I fail at something, I know it is because I . . .
7. When people take advantage of me, I secretly feel . . .
8. When I want to manipulate someone, I . . .
9. At my worst, I am . . .
10. When I am in a bad mood, I . . .
11. The reason I don't like _____ is . . .
12. When I feel insecure, I . . .

What Comes Next?

Congratulations! You've passed the halfway mark in the process of alchemical personal transformation. Shadow work may start out feeling scary, like something dark is lurking around every corner, but once you shine the light of love and compassion on the darkest aspects of yourself, you can move forward with a newfound sense of freedom and self-worth. Congratulate yourself for doing the hard work of uncovering your shadows and take your new self out into the world. The more you present to the rest of the world with your shadows, the more confident and empowered you will feel.

Of course, as with all other phases of personal transformation, shadow work is an ongoing process. If you feel like you're not ready to move on or there are more shadows you need to uncover, you can reread the chapter and rework the exercises until you feel ready. Once you do, you'll begin the next phase of alchemical transformation by entering the Red Phase and engaging in the stage called fermentation.

PART FOUR

The Red Phase

(Fermentation, Distillation, and Coagulation)

Welcome to the final phase of personal transformation, the *Red Phase* or *Rubedo*. In Rubedo, you will continue the work you started in the Black and White Phases. You've begun the process of purification through meditation and worked on forming new self-definitions in order to transform your shadows, polish your golden self to a high shine, and reach the centered balance at the heart of alchemy. In the three stages of the Red Phase, you'll continue to refine and blend aspects of yourself to step into your true power.

CHAPTER 6

Meeting Your Meditative Self Anew

(STAGE 5: FERMENTATION)

In the process of making wine, fermentation occurs when microorganisms convert grapes to wine; it's when interesting things really start to happen. So it is in the alchemy of personal transformation as well. Although you may already be feeling somewhat transformed, this is where the real magic of metamorphosis begins to take place. In this phase, you'll take the raw materials you've created from the first four stages and combine them with your higher self, using meditation and contemplation to emerge as someone altogether different from when you started.

Fermentation Basics

When you're in the fermentation phase, there are several tools you can work with to assist in the process. You can do chakra work and use the corresponding color, crystals, and essential oils in the exercises described later, as well as in your own personalized work.

Associations with fermentation include:

» Purpose: breakdown of inauthentic self and rebirth of authentic self

» Chakra: throat

» Color: blue

» Substance: sulfur

» Crystals and stones: blue lace agate, blue kyanite, iolite, lapis lazuli, sodalite, tanzanite, turquoise

» Essential oils: chamomile, frankincense, eucalyptus

Sitting with Your Meditative Self

You spent a lot of time during conjunction coming into contact with your shadows. You worked on identifying your shadows and simply sitting with them in order to accept and understand more about your subconscious mind and all that you've hidden from the world (and, most likely, yourself). In fermentation, it's time to *do something* with those shadows.

When winemakers ferment grapes, they do so by introducing a single ingredient to the crushed grapes, grape juice, and skins (called the *must*). That ingredient is yeast, and it often naturally finds its way to the must as airborne particles, although it can also be introduced manually. When yeast meets sugars in the must, the sugar is converted to alcohol. With that simple process, grapes become something entirely new.

In fermentation, you'll do something similar. You'll sit with both halves of your whole self—shadow and light—and allow them to mix with a key ingredient in order to become a unified whole that is far more powerful than the sum of its parts.

The process seems almost magical, but it's deliberately created. In alchemical fermentation for personal metamorphoses, the key ingredient is not yeast but contemplation via meditation. This practice not only brings more light to your shadows but also transforms them into something beautiful and new. By returning to contemplation through meditation in this stage, you'll start to see a new sense of self emerging, one that gives you the first true glimpse of who you will be when your transformation is complete.

Do this with kindness, love, and deep self-compassion, avoiding self-criticism or judgment. Listen for the inner voice of judgment (which comes from the small "I") and catch it before it sets in. When you notice you're judging yourself, gently repeat a mantra, such as, "I love myself and am growing into the self I always knew I could be." Do this every time you find yourself judging or criticizing.

Fostering a Meditative Body, Mind, and Spirit

One primary tool of fermentation is meditation, which allows you to delve deeply into self to bring about change. I recommend engaging in a meditative practice once or twice a day for 15 to 20 minutes at a time; about 30 minutes per day is ideal. During this time, allow any thoughts to percolate to the surface without judgment and without actively trying to suppress them. If your mind wanders, gently thank your ego for trying to protect you and return to mindfulness. If things feel stressful, as they can when you're blending your dark and light, breathe deeply as you gently place your hands over your heart and allow their warmth to fill you until you feel calm once again.

For some, this process may trigger unexpected emotions when you're not meditating, as ego struggles to retain its control by reasserting the small "I." When this happens, treat yourself with kindness and love, return to meditation as soon as you're able, and practice the fermentation exercises in this chapter. You can also try talk therapy or counseling to help you process your feelings and emotions. I also highly recommend journaling during this process. Whatever you choose, be patient and allow it to take as long as it takes; you may move through fermentation quickly, or it may take days, weeks, or even months. There's no hurry. The journey is just as important as the destination.

The Magic of Meditation

I'll let you in on a little secret: I spent years—decades, really—being incredibly uncomfortable with meditation. In fact, for the first 30-plus years of my life, I believed I couldn't meditate. As one who has a highly active mind, I found it impossible to sit with myself in the silence. At least, that was what I told myself as I avoided meditation.

What I realize now, from a different place in my life, is that I was uncomfortable with meditation because I was uncomfortable with myself. I grew up in a religious, if somewhat dysfunctional, family, and I was a psychic kid, which made me "weird." As a result, I internalized a lot of messages about how not okay I was at a young age, and by the time I was a teenager, I'd stuffed a lot into my shadows (including my psychic abilities) in order to fit in.

What happened when I meditated was that my true self tried to sneak in, and since I'd so thoroughly disowned that part of myself while seeking the approval of others, sitting in quiet contemplation terrified me. Meditation threatened to shatter the facade of my inauthenticity, so even though I knew it would help me manage some of my anxieties and reach some of my goals, I skipped it, eventually even branding it an impossibility for myself.

Getting Past Meditation Resistance

It wasn't until I was ready to transform and embrace my true self that meditation became my regular practice. Even then, I had to back into it by finding creative ways to quiet my mind. I was able to rekindle my meditative mind through reflective writing. At first, I wrote my truth barely disguised as fiction. This helped me recognize that what I was presenting as fiction was actually the authentic me. Once it was out there, it became easier to inhabit my authentic self.

I find I'm not so unusual in that way. Many people resist meditation, and most feel they have a good reason for doing so. Some reasons people share (and that I've used myself) for resisting meditation include:

» I don't have the time.

» It's so boring!

» I can't clear my mind no matter how hard I try.

» It's too noisy/chaotic/busy at my house.

» It's too "woo-woo."

I know this is true because, in my classes and private sessions, when the topic comes up, a significant number of my healing partners and students look terrified or express distaste at the very thought of developing a regular meditation practice. However, after they do shadow work and realize how much of themselves they've suppressed, the idea of meditation becomes a little less frightening.

If you are resistant to meditation, welcome to the club! You're in good company. I'd like to start by reassuring you that you are completely safe. Meditation won't harm you and will, in fact, make a huge difference in your life. However, if you are someone who can't imagine sitting pretzeled in the lotus position chanting, "I have good news!" That's only one way to meditate, and if it doesn't resonate with you, you can try other methods as well:

» Focus on your breathing. If your attention wanders, return your focus to your breathing.

» Focus on an object, such as a candle flame. When your attention wanders, return your focus to the flame.

» Try movement meditation. Go for a walk or engage in some other repetitive movement (I like dance) and keep your mind focused on the movement of your body. If your thoughts wander, return your focus to the movement.

» Practice daily presence, something I like to call "living meditation." Focus on the sensations of whatever you're doing in the moment. For example, if you're washing your hands, feel the warmth of the water and notice the slipperiness and aroma of the soap. If your mind wanders, return to sensation. If you're eating dinner, notice the flavors, aromas, textures, and sounds of everything that you eat or drink.

» Listen to music and focus on the sounds. If your mind wanders, return it gently to the music.

» Write your truth as fiction, poetry, song lyrics, or straight-up journaling.

These are just a few of the many ways you can meditate that don't involve chanting or sitting; however, you can also engage in chanting mantras and sitting if that works for you. Chant a mantra, such as "Om" (the fundamental sound of the universe according to Hindu scripture) or "Om mani padme hum (a Buddhist mantra of compassion), or choose a simple phrase like "Peace" or "Love." If your attention wanders, return it gently to your mantra.

Why Meditation Works

Each form of meditation works because it takes you out of ego's small "I" and allows you to engage in presence. You are never more authentic than when you are not listening to the ruminations of your ego but are instead allowing yourself to be present in the moment and focused on sensation. During these quiet times, your Divine self, or soul, can communicate with the physical you, making you calmer, more centered, more present, and more able to engage in and enjoy every aspect of your life. The key to fermentation is being present, allowing your Divine self to mix with your human self to transform your shadows to light.

As the process continues, you'll find that what you've struggled with in the past becomes easier, and you'll find it easier to accept all aspects of yourself as you step into the flow of your emerging self.

FERMENTATION EXERCISE #1: **MEDITATION**

Chamomile Tea Throat Chakra Meditation

YOU WILL NEED:

- » **teacup**
- » **boiling water**
- » **chamomile tea**
- » **journal and pen**

➤ Brew a cup of chamomile tea. Allow the tea to cool slightly so you can sip it easily without burning your mouth. Take your cup of tea and go somewhere you won't be disturbed.

➤ Sit comfortably with your hands wrapped around your teacup. Breathe in the steam and aroma from the tea. As you do so, visualize the steam going in through your nose and down into your throat chakra, which is in the center of your throat near your thyroid.

➤ Visualize the steam and aroma from the tea mixing with the spinning blue wheel of light that is your throat chakra. Lift your face away from the teacup and breathe out through your mouth.

➤ Now take a mouthful of tea. As you swallow, visualize the tea flowing down your throat. Feel it as it warms your throat chakra on the way to your stomach. Notice the taste, warmth, and aroma, as well as the sensation of the warm liquid moving down your throat and into your stomach. Remain as focused on sensation as you can.

➤ Continue in this way, first breathing in the steam and then taking a sip, until your tea is gone. If your mind wanders, gently return it to sensation.

➤ When you're done, write your experience in your journal.

Meeting the World with Your Meditative Self

As you become more comfortable with clearing your mind and staying alert and focused in the moment, you'll discover more opportunities to do so. Many people find that as time passes, they become calmer, more present, and less likely to fill their time with the mental noise that comes from ego. This is one of the gifts of fermentation, being able to just *be* without needing to think about it, justify it, or worry about how you're being perceived.

Cultivating presence allows you to relax in many aspects of your life. It lets you enjoy things more thoroughly as you quiet the noise of your mind. You may also notice your relationships become more authentic and peaceful and that you pick and choose activities because you enjoy them or because they're meaningful rather than just because they occupy your time. One of the biggest things I noticed as I cultivated presence was that I was seldom bored, and I spent a lot less time in mindless activities like watching television.

As you grow more peaceful and centered, those around you will notice. Some may be uncomfortable with your newfound peace, but in your new state, you'll recognize their discomfort is about them and not you. It's much easier to be your authentic self with others when you practice presence, and you spend a lot less time trying to earn the approval of others. By engaging in presence, you won't need to internalize aspects of yourself and turn them into new shadows.

Remy spent a lot of time doing what I call "leading with her chin." She always barreled forward, seemingly looking for things to upset or anger her.

During our work together, Remy was in the process of a home remodel, and she was stressed to the max. One entire session was spent with her raging on about how the various contractors were underperforming.

Remy was already aware of this tendency to lead with her chin; we'd discussed it at length before, and it had also come up during her shadow work.

"So how's your meditation going?" I asked after one such session.

"I don't have time for that, plus you know I'm just not good at it," Remy told me.

So Remy and I discussed alternatives to traditional meditation, and she decided she could try practicing presence during her workouts.

The next time I saw her, Remy's entire demeanor had changed. When I asked her what had happened, she told me that one day after practicing being sensation-focused in her workout, it suddenly occurred to her that perhaps her frustration with her subcontractors was occurring because she was expecting to be frustrated.

"I just decided to stop," she told me. "I was creating my own frustration." Moving forward, our sessions changed, and Remy was far less angry and frustrated than I'd ever seen her.

Going with the Flow

YOU WILL NEED:

» **frankincense essential oil and a diffuser or frankincense incense**

» **incense holder and matches (if using incense)**

» **timer**

» **journal and pen**

➤ Go somewhere you won't be disturbed. Put the essential oil in the diffuser and turn it on or light the incense and place it in the holder. Set the timer for 15 to 20 minutes. Sit or lie comfortably.

➤ Think about some aspect of a shadow you've uncovered that still frustrates you. Bring it to mind as vividly as you can, visualizing yourself displaying this trait very publicly. Now imagine that, while still displaying that trait, you come alongside a gently flowing river.

➤ Wade into the water of the river and lie down on your back. Notice how easily you float and how gently the river supports and nourishes you. Feel the water flow around you, filling you with peace. Lie back and, while still visualizing your shadow trait, float down the river peacefully and without self-judgment. Continue to float with your shadow in the river until your timer goes off.

➤ Write your experience in your journal.

SURPASSING ROADBLOCKS

For this journal prompt, you'll need a copy of your responses to the "Surpassing Roadblocks" sidebar in chapter 5 (page 67)—or you can rewrite new answers to the questions (revisited below). Then take those answers and explore the new questions that follow. Working with these questions will help you transform your shadows so you can reintegrate them into your whole self.

1. I don't like _____ about myself.
2. I am afraid others won't like me if I . . .
3. I know others don't like me when I . . .
4. My worst trait is . . .
5. When I display this trait, I feel . . .
6. When I fail at something, I know it is because I . . .
7. When people take advantage of me, I secretly feel . . .
8. When I want to manipulate someone, I . . .
9. At my worst, I am . . .
10. When I am in a bad mood, I . . .
11. The reason I don't like _____ is . . .
12. When I feel insecure, I . . .

Working with one of the questions above at a time, write the following:

1. This trait is also a positive force in my life when I . . .
2. If someone else told me they disliked this about themselves, I would . . .
3. I can love this trait in myself because . . .

What Comes Next?

Congratulations! You've turned from grapes into wine! You've brought light to your shadows, and you're ready to begin refining your new sense of self. If you're still not feeling quite right, feel free to reread the chapter and continue to engage in the meditative practices and fermentation exercises until you feel comfortable and ready to move on. After all, this is a process; there's no need to hurry. Transformation takes time, so be patient and loving with yourself. When you're ready, you can move on to the next stage, which is distillation.

CHAPTER 7

Awakening Your Enlightened Self
(STAGE 6: DISTILLATION)

When a distiller makes spirits, they take the fermented alcohol (which can be wine or beer depending on whether they use fruit or grains) and boil it in a still to purify it. It's an apt metaphor for distillation in our personal transformation as well: you'll take the new self you created during the fermentation phase and purify it with consciousness in order to create a clearer, more enlightened and authentic sense of self. In this chapter, we'll look at how you can continue to purify the new you.

Distillation Basics

When you're in the distillation phase, there are several tools that can assist in the process. You can work with the corresponding elements, chakra, colors, crystals, and oils to create your own distillation rituals. Associations with distillation include:

» Purpose: self-purification, enlightenment, and refinement

» Chakra: third eye

» Colors: violet, indigo

» Substances and elements: mercury, air

» Crystals and stones: charoite, amethyst, sugilite, lepidolite

» Essential oils: lavender, clary sage, marjoram

Celebrating Your Conscious Self

The primary goal of distillation is to move your new self closer to consciousness or enlightenment. To do this, you sit with your higher self and the forces of the Divine in order to blend your embodied self more deeply with Source.

One major difference between an embodied human and Source energy is the experience of duality, where we identify ourselves as separate from everything around us. As discussed earlier, when you embody (agree to become a soul entering a human body), you also agree to the concept of duality, which exists in the physical world but not in Source energy. In other words, you agree to believe in the earthbound illusion of life in a physical, human body.

Think of it like watching a movie. In the back of your mind, you're still aware of who you are, but while you're watching the movie, you choose to suspend that remembrance so you can become immersed in the film you are watching.

Your soul is like the Divine version of your physical self at a movie. In entering your current life, your soul agrees to set aside what you know to be true about yourself—that you are Source energy—so you can have a fully human experience. However, even in your human existence, deep inside you still have knowledge and understanding of yourself as a Divine being.

During the distillation stage of personal metamorphosis, you become more aware of your Divinity in order to move closer to enlightenment. As your embodied self becomes more authentic, the walls of illusion begin to thin, and you start to remember who you truly are.

This is a very cool experience, especially when you first notice it. There's a thinning of the veil between your embodied self and your soul self, and your Divinity begins to slip through from time to time. This can lead to flashes of insight, the recognition of guidance, and moments of incredible clarity.

Being Conscious with Body, Mind, and Spirit

Your third eye chakra, a spinning wheel of violet light in the middle of your forehead, is where you begin to cultivate awareness of your Divine self. It is through your third eye that Divine guidance enters. Guidance can come from a host of sources, including your higher self (your soul), spirit guides, angels, and loved ones who have passed away. It can come in dreams or flashes of insight, during meditation, when you're cultivating presence, during writing exercises, or even spontaneously as you go about daily life.

In the beginning, these flashes of sudden enlightenment, something Japanese Buddhists call *satori*, can be fleeting and difficult to grasp. You'll have a moment of stunning clarity that quickly slips away as you return to your focus on the illusion of duality. However, with time and practice, which is what distillation is all about, you may be able to retain this state for longer, or recall it and deliberately move into it again.

Body

You can engage in a number of body awareness practices that cultivate satori, or what I like to call "body joy." One of my favorites is a form of dance called Nia, which combines various martial arts and dance forms with healing arts. In Nia, you focus on sensation while you move and you cultivate pleasure through the movement by listening to your body's feedback and modifying the practice accordingly. In this way, you remain in a state of pleasurable sensation. Other movement practices that cultivate satori include:

- » yoga
- » tai chi
- » qigong
- » breathwork
- » mindful movement
- » focusing on body sensations throughout the day and seeking out those that are pleasurable instead of painful

- » floating
- » enjoying sensations from food and drink, such as aromas, textures, smells, etc.
- » engaging in any other movement practice, formal or informal, that cultivates body joy

Notice in that last point I said formal or informal; you don't need to take classes to cultivate body joy. Here's a simple exercise to try: Lift your dominant hand in front of you and wriggle your fingers, making "creepy crawly" moves with them. Focus on moving those fingers in a way that is pleasurable and not painful. Now, while continuing to wriggle your fingers, rotate your wrist in a way that feels pleasurable. Add your elbow into the movement and then your upper arm and shoulder, focusing on only pleasurable sensation. If something is painful, then move in a different way that is pleasurable. You can do this throughout your entire body—see how many ways you can move various parts of yourself to cultivate body joy.

Sadly, our contemporary society has moved away from body joy in a way that is harmful to the psyche. In the 1980s, when I was a bodybuilder and aerobics instructor, the philosophy of physical movement was "No pain, no gain." There is a similar belief today that may sound familiar: "Beauty is pain." These damaging beliefs come from ego; we push ourselves physically to the point of pain so that we can meet fabricated societal expectations of physical attractiveness. This is more of our conditioning at play. Engaging in "Beauty is pain" practices harms body, mind, and spirit. I am the owner of creaky knees because of my former insistence on "No pain, no gain," and I spent many of my younger years with a whole lot of food issues, believing that I didn't "deserve" to eat because it would make me fat.

I urge you to engage in physical practices that bring you body joy during your distillation process.

Mind

To cultivate satori in mind, engage in thought exercises that bring you joy. I'm a huge fan of affirmation and visualization, but you can also cultivate mind joy through practices like listening to beautiful music, reading uplifting works such as poetry or spiritual texts, listening to inspiring talks, or engaging in creative pursuits that make you happy. Set aside time for yourself in this way every day so you can get out of your thinking brain and engage with your higher self.

One of my favorite mind joy practices is to sit down with paints and a blank canvas and, with no particular destination or work of art in mind, simply play with color and shape, allowing myself to get lost in the sensation of hue and form. You can also try any of the following:

» Practice stream of consciousness writing with no goal or plan (just write whatever comes to mind).

» Sit down with a musical instrument such as a piano or a kid's xylophone and get lost in tinkering around with it without trying to make a "song" or melody.

» Vocalize in ways that you enjoy without a planned outcome. You can chant nonsense syllables or words you like, hum a tune, or even sing.

» Engage in an absorbing activity such as cooking a meal, kneading bread, knitting, or any other similar hobby you enjoy.

» Make jewelry or string beads, play with sculpting clay, or try other similar arts and crafts.

» Use a guided meditation or visualization.

» Put on headphones and listen to *binaural beats* (tones that stimulate various types of brain waves such as delta or gamma brain waves) or *solfeggio* frequencies (specific healing frequencies that correspond with each chakra). You'll find plenty of phone apps for these.

The goal here is to get you "out of your mind" so spirit can come in and inspire you, and there are as many ways to accomplish this as there are people in the world. My very first experience of getting out of my mind and experiencing satori occurred many decades ago when I was sitting in my backyard in the sunshine and shelling peas. One moment I was there, snapping the peas and smelling their earthy scent, and in the next, I recognized my existence as eternal and outside of space and time. It was beautiful, profound, and spontaneous, and I spent years chasing that experience until I learned to deliberately cultivate it with my own specific practices.

Spirit

Any spiritual practice can cultivate spiritual satori. Here are some examples:

» meditation

» prayer

» mindfulness

» mantras

» self-hypnosis

» chanting

» gratitude practices

You can also cultivate spiritual satori by immersing yourself in beautiful places. Try going to the beach and listening to the crashing of the waves, sitting in your backyard and letting the sun warm you, or walking through the forest.

I like to use a combination of body, mind, and spiritual practices together to bring me into a heightened consciousness. For instance, I might combine simple pleasurable movement practices, such as the creepy crawly hand exercise from page 88, with listening to uplifting music, doing conscious breathwork, and silently listing the things I'm grateful for in my mind. If you're willing to experiment, you can create a practice unique to you, and it can be different every single day.

Getting Satori to Stick Around

In the moments when you finish your practices of body, mind, or spirit and you're feeling blissed out, you will feel clear and connected to Source. However, the moment you return to "regular life," you may find that your state of clarity quickly leaves you. Here is a simple technique from neuro-linguistic programming (NLP, a simple and useful form of self-hypnosis) called *anchoring* that can help you return to satori.

1. When you're in that state of heightened spiritual awareness, create a gesture you don't typically make. For instance, I touch the tip of my middle or ring finger to the tip of my thumb in an "okay" gesture.

2. Hold that gesture until your satori starts to fade, then release it.

3. Any time you wish to return to satori, re-create your gesture and it will return you to that feeling.

You can also program a crystal, such as a piece of clear quartz or amethyst, to hold satori energy. When you're in the blissed-out state, hold the crystal in your dominant hand, which is your giving hand. Visualize the energy of what you feel right now flowing into the crystal for a moment or two. Keep the crystal with you, and when you wish to return to that state, hold it in your nondominant hand, which is your receiving hand, and allow the feeling to return to you.

With both of these practices, I recommend resetting the gesture and reprogramming the crystal every few days to maintain the high, centering energy.

DISTILLATION EXERCISE #1: MEDITATION

Raising Chi on Your Breath

YOU WILL NEED:

» **journal and pen**

This meditation pulls your life force energy from your root chakra (at the base of your spine) through your third eye chakra (in the middle of your forehead) to activate your intuition and facilitate distillation.

➤ Sit or lie comfortably in a place where you won't be disturbed. Breathe in through your nose and out through your mouth to reach a relaxed, meditative state.

1. Inhale through your nose, pulling the air to your root chakra. Visualize the air mixing with the red light of your root chakra. Exhale through your mouth. See the energy from your root chakra flow to your sacral chakra just below and behind your belly button and blend there.

2. Inhale, pulling air to your sacral chakra and mixing with the orange light there. Exhale, visualizing energy flowing to your solar plexus chakra, at the bottom of your sternum, from your sacral chakra.

3. Inhale, pulling air to your solar plexus chakra and mixing with the golden light there. Exhale, visualizing energy flowing to your heart chakra in the center of your chest.

4. Inhale, pulling air to your heart chakra and mixing with the green light there. Exhale, visualizing energy flowing to your throat chakra, in the center of your throat.

5. Inhale, pulling air to your throat chakra and mixing with the blue light there. Exhale, visualizing energy flowing to your third eye chakra.

6. Inhale, pulling air to your third eye chakra and mixing with the violet light there. Exhale, visualizing the violet light suffusing your entire body.

7. Repeat the cycle seven times.

➤ Write your impressions in your journal.

Meeting the World with Your Conscious Self

As you cultivate consciousness, you'll find it changes how you inhabit your embodied experience. Sure, you may still get caught up in the drama of day-to-day life; that's part of being human. But you'll also be aware that there's an eternal, quiet part of you that sits back watchfully and stays peaceful, regardless of what's happening in the world around you. There's a consciousness within you that knows what you're seeing is an illusion and not reality, like watching a movie. The plot is engaging and immersive, but there's another aspect of the real you that's watching everything unfold and enjoying the heck out of it. As you get to know this newly awakened aspect of yourself, you'll find you can step into it whenever you want to return to your center—no matter what is happening around you in your physical existence.

You may also notice that you have more flashes of clarity and insight that occur spontaneously throughout the day. You'll find you are more present, focused, and calmer in all that you do.

You may begin experiencing spontaneous insights during meditative or presence practices. You may also become more aware of an ever-present

FINDING INSPIRATION

A period of worldwide strife had left Isaac feeling anxious in spite of his typically Zen outlook. As he would scroll through the news on his phone, he'd grow more upset with each headline.

Isaac shared this in a session, saying, "I'm usually so Zen, but I feel myself getting upset."

I asked Isaac what he would typically do when he saw an upsetting headline.

"I feel anxious, try to ignore it, and keep scrolling," he told me. "My anxiety ratchets up and up."

I suggested Isaac try sitting with the anxiety whenever it arose instead of ignoring it, just to see what would happen.

In our next session, a surprised Isaac reported back. "I can't believe I forgot about sitting with the feeling and allowing it," he said excitedly. "I just got so caught up in the drama of it all, I forgot I had the tools to deal with this."

Isaac shared that when he sat with the anxiety, he'd feel stressed for a moment or two, but then his higher self would step in, bringing a deep sense of peace. Isaac noted that suppressing the anxiety instead of allowing it caused him to internalize it, which made it persist. By sitting with it, Isaac's higher self was able to step in and set him back on his peaceful path, easing his anxiety and allowing him to view the events from a higher perspective.

guiding voice, like a quiet knowing that underlies all you do. I find that as I move more deeply into distillation, I have more significant and memorable dreams as my guides communicate with me while I sleep and my gut feelings grow stronger.

Breath of Spirit

This exercise helps to further activate your third eye chakra while facilitating clear thinking and connecting you to higher guidance.

YOU WILL NEED:

» **cushion or yoga mat**

» **timer**

» **amethyst crystal**

» **journal and pen**

➤ Sit comfortably on the floor in a place where you won't be disturbed. Set the timer for 15 to 20 minutes. Breathe in through your nose and out through your mouth until you reach a relaxed and meditative state.

➤ Hold the amethyst crystal in your hands. Visualize violet light filled with the wisdom of spirit swirling all around your head. Take a deep breath in through your nose, pulling in the violet light as you breathe in. See the light fill your entire head. Now bring your hands and the crystal up to your mouth and breathe the violet light out into the crystal.

➤ Lie on your back comfortably. Place the amethyst that you've infused with the violet light in the middle of your forehead on your third eye chakra. Continue breathing in through your nose and out through your mouth as you lie with the amethyst on your forehead. See the violet light from the amethyst beaming into your third eye chakra and filling your entire being. Continue this visualization until your timer goes off.

➤ Take the amethyst off your head and sit up. Visualize roots growing from your root chakra down into the earth below you in order to ground yourself.

➤ When you're done, write your experiences in your journal.

This journal prompt is different from others. Instead of answering a series of questions, as you have in the past, you will engage in the process of continuous writing.

Set a timer for 20 minutes. Take a deep breath in and visualize yourself surrounded by violet light that fills your entire body and aura. When you're enveloped in the violet light, start writing in your journal.

Begin by writing the words "In the violet light of spirit, I . . ." Then continue writing without trying to edit or control what you write. Allow the words to flow from your pen onto the page without censoring or worrying about what you're writing; this should be stream of consciousness.

If you get stuck or your mind goes blank, simply continue to write the last word you wrote until you unstick and move on. Do this without any criticism or judgment. Don't worry about spelling, punctuation, grammar, or even making it sound "right." Just write until your timer goes off, and then read what you have written.

Alternatively, you can write, "In the violet light of spirit, I draw . . ." and then allow your pen or pencil to move across the page without worrying about trying to draw anything specific; simply allow your pen to move.

What Comes Next?

In distillation, you'll begin to have moments of such lovely clarity that you'll want to chase them so you can have more. It's a beautiful phase that's a lot of fun, and your golden self is really starting to reveal itself now. As always, this is a process, so be kind, compassionate, and patient with yourself. You're welcome to remain in this phase as long as you wish or need, rereading the chapter or reworking the exercises until you're ready to move on. When you are, you'll begin the final phase of revealing your golden and centered self, which is coagulation.

CHAPTER 8

Becoming Your Centered Self

(STAGE 7: COAGULATION)

Whether you've been at the process of metamorphosis for days, weeks, months, or even years, it all comes down to coagulation. This is where you reveal the golden center that was with you all along, buried by layers of conditioning, ego, and the small "I." And what a beautiful thing that is, finding your core of gold that you've hidden from yourself and others for so long. In this phase, it will finally be revealed.

Coagulation Basics

When you're in the coagulation phase, there are several tools you can use to assist in the process. Work with your crown chakra as well as the corresponding colors, crystals, and essential oils to facilitate your coagulation work. Associations with coagulation include:

» Purpose: revealing your golden self

» Chakra: crown

» Colors: white, clear, gold

» Substances and elements: gold; balance of earth, air, fire, and water

» Crystals and stones: clear quartz, phenacite, selenite, apophyllite

» Essential oils: jasmine, sandalwood, rosewood, palo santo

Finding Your Golden Center

What a journey you have taken, from that old self so wrapped up in the illusion of being human that you had forgotten your own Divinity to where you are now. Each step of the way, you have persevered. You've delved deeply into your shadows, discovered your conditioning, and expanded from the small "I" of ego to pursue your true glory as a Divine being. You've worked to balance elemental energies, blending them to become a whole that is so much greater than the sum of its parts. You've faced your shadows head-on and loved them into the light. You're now poised to rediscover something you probably weren't even aware you lost: your golden self.

Take a moment to pause here and reflect on the journey—not in a way that is judgmental or critical of who you once were, but in a manner that celebrates and honors your drive for authenticity and your travels through the previous six stages of alchemical personal transformation. Reflecting in this way reminds you of something very important: each step toward your golden self has revealed just how powerful, beautiful, and resilient you truly are, and now it's time to polish up that golden center and unveil it to the world.

Expanding your small "I" into your gorgeous golden self is the work of a lifetime, and it's one you'll embark upon more than once, because there's always another facet of your golden self to find and reveal, no matter your age, gender, or other aspects. Personal transformation is like an onion; as you move through your life's journey into the most expansive form of yourself, you'll find there's layer after layer of you, each with its own golden center just waiting to be revealed.

All humans are like that; each of us is our own unique and beautiful self, like a *matryoshka* (Russian nesting doll). With each layer we expose, we reveal a self that's more expansive than the one before. Ironically, in stripping away the layers of self, we don't become smaller; indeed, we become larger and more connected to the wisdom and power of the Divine. We also have so much less baggage that we can move forward with a lightness and freedom we may once have thought impossible. As we polish layer after layer of tarnish created by conditioning and ego, we get closer to the Source from which we came and to which we will return.

So how do you finally reveal this beautiful new you that was there all along? You do it through the process of mixing, blending, combining, and balancing all that you've worked with in each stage. This is your Magnum Opus and your Great Work finally ready to see the light of day, and you can feel comfortable sharing it with others because of all of the work you've done so far.

Creating Your Centered Self

In each of the previous stages, you've worked with a single element to reveal a different aspect of self that was hidden from you and others by ego and conditioning. In coagulation, however, you bring all of that together into a balance that harmoniously blends the elements of earth, air, fire, and water and merges body, mind, and spirit into a unified whole, rather than viewing each as a separate entity. Put simply, this is where it all comes together.

Coagulation calls for you to recognize that although you *can* separate yourself into your various elemental energies of earth, air, fire, and water and you *can* look after body, mind, and spirit separately, when you work with each aspect of self as part of a unified whole, you can live from a place of empowerment and balance that combines the earthly, embodied you with the energy that makes up your very soul. Coagulation allows you to remain embodied while also rejoining with Source energy, which is your birthright. In coagulation, you finally remember (in body, mind, and spirit) who you truly are, and you can carry that awareness with you throughout your life, regardless of what is happening within the embodied experience.

This is your true Source of empowerment. For most of your life, the ego has told you that you have to do so many things to have the small "I" be worthy of love. In coagulation, you finally realize that by simply being, you are not only worthy of unconditional love but also deeply and power-fully loved every step of the way. You don't have to be anything other than exactly who you are.

Blending Body, Mind, and Spirit

To blend body, mind, and spirit into a whole, start viewing yourself holisti-cally and engaging each of these parts in everything you do. To do this, use your internal guidance (some call it gut feelings or intuition) as a barome-ter, telling you whether something serves your greatest good. If something serves the greatest good of body, mind, and spirit, then you feel a sense of rightness within you. If something doesn't serve you, then something feels "off." It's as simple as that.

If you're out of balance, you'll experience a symptom, whether it's a bodily pain, a negative thought, or a sense of spiritual discord. Pay atten-tion to each symptom. Sit with it, ask what it's trying to tell you, and then seek balance again. Listen to your guidance; it will serve you well.

As you meld body, mind, and spirit, you'll also need to set aside things like judgment and criticism and replace them with the understanding that nothing is inherently good or inherently bad; it all just is. That doesn't mean you ignore good judgment and flail about. Instead of asking your-self, "Is this good or bad?" or "Is this positive or negative?" ask, "Does this serve my highest good?" The highest good doesn't involve causing harm to others or stepping on someone else in order to elevate yourself. If you feel a rightness inside, chances are you're headed in the direction that, in this moment, is the right one for you.

Enjoy the journey for its own sake. You don't need to have a destination in mind; just keep pursuing joy, love, compassion, and peace. You don't have to be so self-directed that you only move in a straight line. Blending body, mind, and spirit allows you to wander, learn, and explore simply for the sake of discovery and personal joy. For a while, you may travel purposefully along one road until spirit whispers in your ear, "Turn left." Listen to the urging of your intuition; it's there to guide you toward your highest good at all times. Your highest good can change from moment to moment, so keep following the urgings of your soul with a spirit of curiosity and without an agenda.

The other way to balance body, mind, and spirit is to recognize that what you do to one component affects the other two. What you choose to eat affects not just your body but also your mind and spirit, so choose consciously in a manner that suits your personal values in that moment. What you choose to think affects not just your mind but also your spirit and your body, so choose thoughts that support all three. Spiritual practice affects not just your soul but also your body and mind, so choose practices that will nourish those as well. When one is out of balance, an imbalance in the other two will also occur. Use the wisdom of your golden self to return to your center in order to bring the balance you need.

Balancing Earth, Air, Fire, and Water

Whereas energy in the physical world can split up into earth, air, fire, and water, in Source it is all one thing. In the embodied experience, earth, air, fire, and water are the "humors" that can become unbalanced if you don't continuously seek harmony. If you notice symptoms of being out of balance (we discussed them in chapter 1 on pages 9 and 10), use the opposite energy to bring yourself back into balance, remembering this:

» Fire balances water and water balances fire.

» Earth balances air and air balances earth.

The trick is learning to recognize when one element has become too weak or too dominant and then introducing its opposite or fortifying it to bring harmony. Return to chapter 1 if you need a refresher on what each element out of balance looks like.

Earth, Air, Fire, Water

The full moon offers the perfect opportunity for personal and energetic cleansing. This exercise combines all four elements while allowing you to renew yourself and your energy.

YOU WILL NEED:

- » **water bottle filled with water**
- » **four clear quartz crystal points**
- » **palo santo wood or cedar wood**
- » **matches**
- » **journal and pen**

➤ On the night before the full moon, place the water bottle out in the moonlight (or on a windowsill) and place each of the crystal points around the base of the water bottle, touching it. This infuses the water with moonlight energy and crystal (earth) energy.

➤ On the night of the full moon, light your palo santo or cedar wood and allow it to burn until it smolders and smokes. As it burns, repeat the mantra "Fire ignites my golden self."

➤ Beginning at your front door, walk the outside perimeter of your house, blowing on the palo santo or cedar wood to spread the smoke all around your house.

➤ When you return to the front door, use your hands to fan the palo santo or cedar wood smoke over your crown chakra (at the top of your head), visualizing it flowing down through your crown and into your entire aura and body. As you do so, repeat the mantra "Air reveals my golden self."

➤ Extinguish the palo santo or cedar wood and drink your moonlight-infused water, thinking to yourself, "Water cleanses my golden self."

➤ Stand with your bare feet on the grass and visualize roots growing into the ground. As you do so, repeat the mantra "Earth nourishes my golden self."

➤ When you're done, write your experiences in your journal.

Meeting the World as Your Centered Self

When you are centered and balanced, you'll notice all sorts of things happening:

» You'll feel like you're in the "flow" of life; things will shift and change, and you'll easily move with each.

» You'll feel more peaceful.

» You'll live with more compassion for self and others.

» Your thoughts, words, and actions will come from love.

» You'll live more intuitively and harmoniously.

» You'll be less reactive to the world around you.

» You'll be less judgmental of self and others.

» When something comes up, you'll return to your center much more quickly and easily.

» You'll have better control of your thoughts.

» Your ego won't exert as much control; instead, it will become a tool you use for growth.

» You'll be more satisfied with the simple things in life.

» You will gain clarity about your life's direction.

Please remember as you contemplate these things, however, that you are still a human being, and there will be times when you get caught up in the drama of human experience. However, at some point your golden self will step back in and remind you to live from your center, and you'll be able to step away from the drama much more easily and quickly than you have in the past.

Living in the world from your golden self doesn't just benefit you; it benefits everyone in your life and the universe as a whole. When you live from a centered place, you hold space for higher energy that affects those around you. When your energy has a higher vibration (which is the ultimate result of living as your golden self), it raises the vibration of the universe as a whole. In this way, doing your work becomes the work of humanity, as we all work together to move closer to Source energy.

Likewise, you'll be an inspiration to others, and you won't even need to try. Others will notice your calm centeredness. Some might find it threatening and react negatively to it because of where they are in their own

FINDING INSPIRATION

Mari loved her stepchild, but she'd always had a difficult relationship with Michael, as stepmothers and stepchildren often do. When Michael was young, they sometimes butted heads, and each occasionally resented the other.

One day, adult Michael disappeared from Mari's life. No phone calls. No visits. No texts. Mari worried something was wrong—perhaps the resentment had grown and Michael was lost to her forever.

Mari was in the process of transformation, so each night in her mind and prayers she sent Michael love, hoping for contact someday soon.

After about a year, Mari decided to text and invite Michael to join in on a family trip. She heard nothing for days, but she continued to send love.

After about a week, Mari received a text from her stepchild. Michael apologized for being out of touch and explained there had been a transformation: Mari's son Michael was now her daughter Emily, and she was ready to return to the embrace of family.

It was big news, but Mari felt only peace in knowing that their child would return to her, resentment-free and as her true self.

Some in Mari's family were uncomfortable with the change, but Mari continued to hold them all in love, allowing each their own process. When the family traveled together, it was a joyful reunion, and Mari's relationship with her stepdaughter was as transformed as both Mari and Emily were.

processes, but your golden self will remind you that's their stuff and not yours. You'll be able to either be compassionately supportive or to lovingly step away for your own peace of mind.

Others will want what you have and ask you how you got it. The greatest gift you can give is to point them in the direction of their own transformation, allowing them to find their way to it as you found yours. While they do, you can be there to support them. Hold space for them by providing a soft and peaceful place to land as they pursue the often tumultuous path of their own growth. You can bear witness to their transformation without needing to control or judge it. Your love will be their strength and support.

COAGULATION EXERCISE #2: **MEDITATION**

4 Element, 7 Chakra Balancing Visualization

YOU WILL NEED:

» **journal and pen**

➤ This meditation is the culmination of your cycle of alchemy. It combines earth, air, fire, and water as you balance your chakras.

➤ Go somewhere you won't be disturbed. If you can do this exercise outside on the lawn or in nature under a tree, do so. Otherwise, do it inside. Sit comfortably. Close your eyes and breathe deeply in through your nose and out through your mouth.

➤ When you are in a meditative state, bring your focus to where your bottom meets the earth. Feel the energy of the earth supporting you completely. Imagine drawing the energy of the earth up through your root chakra, at the base of your spine, and traveling up through each chakra in turn until it reaches your crown.

➤ Now imagine a breeze blowing all around you. Breathe in the breeze and visualize it filling your lungs, moving through your heart, and spreading through your body with every beat of your heart.

➤ Imagine sunlight now, warming and pure, soaking into you through your skin and warming your bones, muscles, and organs until you are infused with the light.

➤ Finally, imagine a waterfall above your head, pouring water down through your crown chakra, flowing down each chakra in turn, and cleansing you until it pours out and into the earth.

➤ Sit for as long as you wish, feeling deep peace. When you're ready, open your eyes.

➤ When you're done, write your experiences in your journal.

This is a journal prompt that also involves a little visualization. It's a great way to get unstuck and facilitate your growth through the balance of chakras and elements.

1. Close your eyes and put your bare feet on the ground. Feel the earth support and nourish you. Write what you notice.

2. Take a cooling drink of water or take a warm bath or shower (or dip your bare feet in a stream or the ocean). Write what you notice.

3. Sit in the warmth of sunlight (if it's not sunny, sit by a fire or even a candle flame). Pay attention to the warmth on your skin. Write what you notice.

4. Fan yourself or sit near a breeze, paying attention to the sensation of the breeze. Write what you notice.

5. Focus your attention on your root and sacral chakras (body). Write what you notice.

6. Focus your attention on your solar plexus, heart, and throat chakras (mind). Write what you notice.

7. Focus your attention on your third eye and crown chakras (spirit). Write what you notice.

8. Focus your attention first on your body and then on the space around your body. Shift your focus back and forth between the two. Write what you notice.

Conclusion

Keep Doing Your Own Great Work

Welcome to you! You have journeyed from the small "I" to your expansive, open, free, and centered golden self, and that is cause for celebration. You have become your own Magnum Opus—your own Great Work—and you have earned the right to stand back and admire your magnificence.

Where you go from here is up to you and up to your spirit. As I've discovered from doing this work over and over again, although you are your own Great Work in this moment, there's another moment, and another, and another ad infinitum. Each moment is an opportunity to discover something new. Each holds within it the chance to uncover a new golden self. Each moment is ripe with the possibility of creating a new Magnum Opus that's even more glorious than the one before.

The Great Work is never done. There's always another nesting doll waiting beneath this one, and the new matryoshka is even more beautiful and laden with possibility than the one that covers it.

It's not that you're incomplete as you are. You're not. You are always whole, even when you are the smallest, most ego-driven, and most fearful version of yourself. Rather, you're doing the work of being human. With each new iteration of your Magnum Opus, you accomplish what you incarnated into a human body to do—you grow, shift, change, and move closer to the Source. Your Magnum Opus isn't just the work of a lifetime; it's the work of many lifetimes, in which you explore, play, polish, and shine in this dance of being human.

You have every moment of every day to choose who you are, and there are endless opportunities to find new iterations of self that explore different aspects of duality; you won't stop until you've been them all. Each time you return to a human body, you do so eagerly, joyfully, and in anticipation of the new adventures you'll have this time around.

Round and round and round we go. We explore and play. We try on identities and discard them. Sometimes we get caught up in the illusion for a while because the drama of it all is just so delicious. But in the end, every single one of us will return to our golden self, that great big beautiful soul that lives, dies, laughs, cries, loves, and fears; the one that hides from self only to rediscover who we are over and over again in an endless cycle until we rejoin with Source.

I wish you joy, peace, love, and compassion on your journey.

Glossary

affirmation: A positive statement about something you'd like to see in your life; an "I am" statement

Albedo: Another name for the White Phase

alchemy: A set of concepts and processes that gives you the tools to bring about the growth and transformation you want in your life; the art of transformation

anchoring: A technique that involves using a gesture to program a sensation in order to return to it; from neuro-linguistic programming (NLP)

authentic self: The real you that exists beyond ego and conditioning

Black Phase: The first phase of alchemy, consisting of calcination and dissolution

calcination: The first stage of alchemy; removing the false sense of self

chakras: Seven energy centers that connect body and mind to emotions and spirit

coagulation: The final stage of alchemy; involves revealing the golden self

conjunction: The fourth stage of alchemy; integrating new thoughts and beliefs

dissolution: The second stage of alchemy; involves meditation and going with the flow

distillation: The sixth stage of alchemy; purification

duality: The breaking of energy into opposites, such as dark and light or good and evil

ego: The aspect of personality that forms and protects a sense of identity and individuality

fermentation: The fifth stage of alchemy; involves meeting your meditative self

four classical elements: Energy broken into humors; earth, air, fire, and water

golden self: The ultimate objective of personal transformation; the revealing of your highest self

Great Work: Magnum Opus; the work of alchemy

Magnum Opus: The work of alchemy; the golden self

mantra: A repeated statement chanted or thought in contemplation, such as "Om"

meditation: Practicing presence and contemplation in a ritualistic way

Nigredo: Another name for the Black Phase; the first phase of alchemy, consisting of calcination and dissolution

persona: An archetype of self we present to the world; the ego-driven self

philosopher's stone: The magical substance required for alchemical transformation

prima materia: The starting materials of alchemy; in this case, you

Red Phase: The final phase of alchemy, consisting of fermentation, distillation, and coagulation

Rubedo: Another name for the Red Phase

satori: Sudden enlightenment

separation: The third stage of alchemy; separating false beliefs from truths

shadows: Parts of self you have repressed or disowned

small "I": The self created by ego and conditioning; not your true self

visualization: A meditative activity in which you imagine yourself in some way

White Phase: The second phase of alchemy, consisting of separation and conjunction

Resources

Alcantara, Margarita. *Chakra Healing: A Beginner's Guide to Self-Healing Techniques that Balance the Chakras* (2017). Continue your chakra work with this great beginner's guide, which provides everything you need to know about your chakras.

Cunningham, Scott. *Earth, Air, Fire, and Water: More Techniques of Natural Magic* (2002). Discover practical magical rituals using the four classical elements and learn more about each.

Durn, Sarah. *The Beginner's Guide to Alchemy: Practical Lessons and Exercises to Enhance Your Life* (2020). Learn, play, and discover alchemy in this great guide for beginners.

Frazier, Karen. *Crystals for Beginners: The Guide to Get Started with the Healing Power of Crystals* (2017). Continue your work with crystals and learn how you can use them to heal body, mind, and spirit.

HealingCrystals.com. This is a great website where you can find virtually any crystal you need online, all sustainably sourced.

Worwood, Valier Ann. *The Complete Book of Essential Oils and Aromatherapy* (2016). Learn the basics of essential oils, including how to use them safely and in healing rituals.

References

American Heart Association. "Stress and Heart Health." Accessed October 14, 2020. www.heart.org/en/healthy-living/healthy-lifestyle /stress-management/stress-and-heart-health.

Boyes, Alice. "Avoidance Coping." *Psychology Today*. May 5, 2013. www .psychologytoday.com/us/blog/in-practice/201305 /avoidance-coping.

Editors of *Encyclopaedia Britannica*. "Persona." Britannica. Accessed October 14, 2020. www.britannica.com/science/persona -psychology.

Kübler-Ross, Elisabeth. *On Death and Dying*. London: Taylor & Francis, 2009. New York: The Macmillan Company, 1969.

Mayo Clinic. "Denial: When It Helps, When It Hurts." April 9, 2020. www.mayoclinic.org/healthy-lifestyle/adult-health/in-depth/denial /art-20047926.

Principe, Lawrence M. "The Secrets of Alchemy." Science History Institute. January 29, 2013. www.sciencehistory.org/distillations /the-secrets-of-alchemy.

Sisgold, Steve. "Conscious and Unconscious Regression." *Psychology Today*. September 11, 2014. www.psychologytoday.com/us/blog /life-in-body/201409/conscious-and-unconscious-regression.

Stanford Encyclopedia of Philosophy. "Empedocles." September 26, 2019. Last modified April 7, 2020. plato.stanford.edu/entries /empedocles/.

Index

A

Affirmation, 11, 113
Air, *ix*, 9. *See also* White Phase
Albedo, 43, 113
Alchemical transformation, 4, 15, 18,
    19, 23, 31, 38, 45, 57, 68, 114
Alchemist, greeting your inner, *viii–ix*
Alchemy, *viii*, 113
  beginnings of, 4
  definition, 3
  personal, *ix*, 1
  physical process, *ix*
  seven stages of, 1, 4–8
  use of, 4
American Heart Association, 25
Amethyst, 86, 91, 94, 96
Anchoring, 90, 113
Angels, 10, 87
Astrology, 4, 9
Authentic self, 8, 113
  in body, 49–50
  finding way to, 49
  how to be, 46–49
  in mind, 50
  sharing your, 52
  in spirit, 50–51
Avoidance
  ego's defense mechanism, 21, 32–33
  recognizing, 34

B

Being honest with yourself,
    dissolution, 5–6
Binaural beats, 89
Blackness, 15. *See also*
  Black Phase

Black Phase, 15, 113
  calcination, 15, 17–27
  dissolution, 15, 31–41
  Nigredo, 15, 114
Body
  authenticity in, 49–50
  being conscious with, 87–88
  blending mind, spirit and, 102–103
  growing your, 11
  meditative, 75–78
  sparking the fire of calcination in, 22
Boyes, Alice, 34
Breath of Spirit, visualization
    exercise, 94, 96

C

Calcination, 1, 17, 113
  basics of, 18
  Black Phase, 17–27
  Crystal Fire Meditation,
    meditation exercise, 23–24
  ego's role in, 19–21
  finding inspiration, 25
  igniting incident as impetus
    for change, 19
  life changes from, 23
  meeting the world with
    your fiery self, 24
  recognizing igniting incidents, 18–19
  Root Chakra Awakening,
    visualization exercise, 26
  sparking the fire in body,
    mind, and spirit, 21–23
  sparking your fire, 18–21
  stage of alchemy, 5, 17
  surpassing roadblocks, 27

Centered self
  blending body, mind, and
    spirit, 102–103
  creating your, 101–103
Chakras, 12, 113
  Root Chakra Awakening,
    visualization exercise, 26
  tool for transformation, 12
Chamomile Tea Throat Chakra
    Meditation, meditation
    exercise, 78–79
Classical elements, ix, 9, 114
Cleansing Waterfall, visualization
    exercise, 40
Coagulation, 1, 113
  basics of, 100
  creating your centered self, 8, 101–103
  Earth, Air, Fire, Water, ritual
    exercise, 104
  finding inspiration, 106
  finding your golden center, 100–101
  4 Element, 7 Chakra Balancing
    Visualization, meditation
    exercise, 107–108
  meeting world as centered
    self, 105, 107
  stage of alchemy, 8, 99
  surpassing roadblocks, 109
Conjunction, 1, 57, 113
  basics of, 58
  Earth-Shadow Heart Chakra
    Visualization, visualization
    exercise, 66
  finding inspiration, 65
  knowing shadows of body,
    mind and spirit, 60–63
  Nourishing Your Shadows with
    Earth, ritual exercise, 63–64
  ongoing process of shadow
    work, 59, 67–68
  sharing space with your
    shadow, 58–60
  sharing your shadow self, 64
  stage of alchemy, 6–7

  surpassing roadblocks, 67
Conscious self. See also Distillation
  celebrating your, 86–87
  meeting world with, 92, 94
Coping mechanism
  avoidance, 34
  denial, 33
  doubt, 34–35
  regression, 34
Crystal Fire Meditation, meditation
    exercise, 23–24
Crystals, 18, 32, 46, 56, 74, 86, 100
  amethyst, 86, 91, 94, 96
  Breath of Spirit, visualization
    exercise, 94
  calcite, 32, 46, 58
  Earth, Air, Fire, Water, ritual
    exercise, 104
  healing, 50
  HealingCrystals.com, 115
  programming, 91
  quartz, 23, 32, 58, 63–64, 91, 100, 104
  Solar Plexus Activation,
    meditation exercise, 54
  tourmaline, 18, 58

D

Defense mechanisms,
  recognizing ego's, 21
Denial, recognizing, 33
Displacement, ego's defense
  mechanism, 21
Dissociation, ego's defense
  mechanism, 21
Dissolution, 1, 31, 113
  basics of, 32
  being honest with yourself, 32–35
  Cleansing Waterfall,
    visualization exercise, 40
  embracing your honest body,
    mind and spirit, 35–38
  finding inspiration, 39
  meeting the world with
    your honest self, 38

stage of alchemy, 5–6, 31
surpassing roadblocks, 41
Water Scrying, meditation
	exercise, 37–38
Distillation, 1, 83, 113
	basics of, 86
	being conscious with body,
		mind and spirit, 87–91
	Breath of Spirit, visualization
		exercise, 94, 96
	celebrating your conscious
		self, 86–87
	cultivating satori (body joy), 87–88
	cultivating satori in mind, 89–90
	cultivating spiritual satori, 90
	finding inspiration, 93
	getting satori to stick around, 90–91
	meeting world with conscious
		self, 92, 94
	Rising Chi on Your Breath,
		meditation exercise, 91–92
	stage of alchemy, 8, 85
	surpassing roadblocks, 95
Divine self, 8, 78, 87
Doubt
	forms of, 35
	recognizing, 34–35
Duality, 111, 113
	concept of, 86
	illusion of, 87
	separation and, 7

E

Earth, *ix*, 9
Earth, Air, Fire, Water, ritual
	exercise, 104
Earth-Shadow Heart Chakra
	Visualization, visualization
	exercise, 66
Ego, 113
	avoidance as coping mechanism, 34
	calcination, 5
	denial as coping mechanism, 33
	doubt as coping mechanism, 34–35

experience of, 21
finding inspiration, 25
recognizing defense
	mechanisms, 21, 32–35
regression as coping mechanism, 34
role in calcination, 19–21
Empedocles, 9
Encyclopaedia Britannica, 47
Energy
	air, 9
	balancing earth, air, fire,
		and water, 103
	classical elements, 9–10
	earth, 9
	fire, 9–10
	water, 10
Essential oils
	calcination, 18, 26
	coagulation, 100
	conjunction, 58
	dissolution, 32, 37–38
	distillation, 86
	fermentation, 74, 81
	separation, 46
Exercise(s)
	Breath of Spirit visualization, 94, 96
	Chamomile Tea Throat Chakra
		Meditation meditation, 78–79
	Cleansing Waterfall visualization, 40
	Crystal Fire Meditation
		meditation, 23–24
	Earth, Air, Fire, Water ritual, 104
	Earth-Shadow Heart Chakra
		Visualization visualization, 66
	4 Element, 7 Chakra Balancing
		Visualization meditation, 107–108
	Going with the Flow meditation, 81
	I Am Breathwork meditation, 51–52
	Nourishing Your Shadows with
		Earth ritual, 63–64
	Rising Chi on Your Breath
		meditation, 91–92
	Root Chakra Awakening
		visualization, 26

Exercise(s) (*continued*)
  Solar Plexus Activation
    meditation, 54
  Water Scrying meditation, 37–38

F

Fermentation, 1, 114
  basics of, 74
  Chamomile Tea Throat Chakra
    Meditation, meditation
    exercise, 78–79
  finding inspiration, 80
  fostering a meditative body,
    mind and spirit, 75–78
  getting past meditation
    resistance, 76–78
  Going with the Flow,
    meditation exercise, 81
  magic of meditation, 76
  meditation, 78
  meeting the world with your
    meditative self, 79
  sitting with your meditative
    self, 74–75
  stage of alchemy, 7–8, 73
  surpassing roadblocks, 82
Fire, *ix*, 9–10
4 Element, 7 Chakra Balancing
    Visualization, meditation
    exercise, 107–108
Freud, Sigmund, 34

G

Getting to know your shadows,
    conjunction, 6–7
Going with the Flow, meditation
    exercise, 81
Golden self, *ix*, 45, 57, 96, 114
  Earth, Air, Fire, Water, ritual
    exercise, 104
  ego's defense mechanisms, 33
  finding your, 100–101
  living as your, 105, 107
  polishing your, 11–12, 71

returning to your, 111–112
  tools for, 11–12
Great Work, 8, 101, 111, 114
Greek philosophy, 4, 9
Growth
  body, 11
  bringing alchemical self into world, 11
  mind, 10
  spirit, 10

H

Heart disease, stress as
    contributor, 25
Honesty
  avoidance, 34
  being honest with yourself, 32–35
  contemplation, 35–36
  denial, 33
  doubt, 34–35
  nonjudgment, 36
  overcoming ego's defense
    mechanisms, 35
  recognizing ego's defense
    mechanisms, 32–35
  regression, 34
  unconditional self-love, 36–37

I

I Am Breathwork, meditation
    exercise, 51–52
Inauthenticity, 7, 46–49
  in body, 49
  meditation and, 76
  in mind, 50
  recognizing, 48–49
Inspiration, finding, 13, 25, 39,
    53, 65, 80, 93, 106

J

Journaling. *See also*
    Exercise(s)
  self-observation, 27
  transformation tool, 12
Jung, Carl, 47

K

Kübler-Ross, Elisabeth, 33

M

Magnum Opus, 8, 101, 111, 114
Mantras, 11, 114
Matryoshka (Russian nesting
    doll), 101, 111
Mayo Clinic, 33
Meditation, *viii*, 11, 114
  Chamomile Tea Throat Chakra
    Meditation exercise, 78–79
  Crystal Fire Meditation
    exercise, 23–24
  4 Element, 7 Chakra Balancing
    Visualization exercise, 107–108
  getting past resistance to, 76–78
  Going with the Flow exercise, 81
  I Am Breathwork exercise, 51–52
  magic of, 76
  process of, 78
  reasons for resisting, 76
  Rising Chi on Your Breath
    exercise, 91–92
  Solar Plexus Activation exercise, 54
  tool for transformation, 11
  Water Scrying exercise, 37–38
Meditative self
  fostering body, mind and
    spirit, 75–78
  meeting the world with, 79
  sitting with your, 74–75
Metamorphosis
  Black Phase kickstarting, 15
  path of, 13
Mind
  authenticity in, 50
  being conscious with, 89–90
  blending body, spirit and, 102–103
  growing your, 10
  meditative, 75–78
  sparking the fire of calcination in, 22
Modern alchemy, 4

Must, 74
Mysticism, 4

N

Neuro-linguistic programming
    (NLP), 90, 113
Nigredo, 15, 114. *See also* Black Phase
Nourishing Your Shadows with
    Earth, ritual exercise, 63–64

O

On Death and Dying (Kübler-Ross), 33
Oneness, 7, 10, 20–21, 59

P

Persona, 114
  authentic self and, 48, 49
  term, 47
Personal transformation, *viii–ix*.
    See also Transformation
  calcination, 5
  conjunction, 6–7
  dissolution, 5–6
  growth, 10–11
  ongoing process of shadow
    work, 59, 60, 68
  path of metamorphosis, 13
  returning shadows to light, 60
  separation, 6
  tools for, 11–12
  use of alchemy for, 4
Philosopher's stone, 8, 114
Prima materia, 8, 114
Projection, ego's defense
    mechanism, 21
Psychology, 4
Psychology Today (magazine), 34

Q

Quartz, 23, 32, 58, 63–64, 91, 100, 104

R

Rationalization, ego's defense
    mechanism, 21

Red Phase, 68, 71, 114
  coagulation, 71, 99–109
  distillation, 71, 85–96
  fermentation, 71, 73–83
Reframing, viii
Regression, recognizing, 34
Repression/suppression, ego's
    defense mechanism, 21
Rising Chi on Your Breath,
    meditation exercise, 91–92
Ritual
  Earth, Air, Fire, Water
    exercise, 104
  Nourishing Your Shadows with
    Earth exercise, 63–64
Roadblocks, surpassing, 13, 27,
    41, 55, 67, 82, 95, 109
Root Chakra Awakening,
    visualization exercise, 26
Rubedo, 114. See also Red Phase

S

Satori, 90–91, 114
  body, 87–88
  Japanese Buddhists, 87
  mind, 89–90
  spirit, 90
Selfie, social media phenomenon, 49
Self-love, 35, 36–37, 41, 48, 65
Self-purification, distillation, 8
Self-realization, viii
Separation, 1, 45, 114
  basics of, 46
  being authentic about who
    you are, 46–49
  being authentic in body, mind
    and spirit, 49–51
  finding inspiration, 53
  I Am Breathwork, meditation
    exercise, 51–52
  sharing your authentic self, 52
  Solar Plexus Activation,
    meditation exercise, 54

stage of alchemy, 6
surpassing roadblocks, 55
Shadows, 114
  how they came to be, 59–60
  learning to share space with, 58–60
  returning, to light, 60
  subconscious, 7, 57
Shadow self
  body shadow, 61
  conjunction, 6–7
  from your mind, 62
  sharing, 64
  spiritual shadows, 62–63
Small "I", 20, 114
  centered self, 102, 111
  defense in protecting, 32–33, 35
  expanding your, 100
  inner voice of judgment, 75
  meditation, 78
  values supporting, 59
Solar Plexus Activation,
    meditation exercise, 54
Solfeggio frequencies, 89
Sparking the fire
  in body, mind, and spirit, 21–23
  calcination, 5
Spirit
  authenticity in, 50–51
  being conscious with, 90
  blending body, mind and, 102–103
  growing your, 10
  meditative, 75–78
  sparking the fire of
    calcination in, 22–23
Spirit guides, 10, 87
Stress, heart disease contributor, 25
Subconscious, shadows, 7

T

Tools
  chakras, 12
  journaling, 12
  mantras, 11

meditation, 11
visualizations, 12
Transformation
alchemical, 15, 18, 19, 23, 31,
    38, 45, 57, 68, 114
calcination, 18–23
chakra work, 12
coagulation, 100–101, 107
conjunction, 57, 60, 67–68
dissolution, 31–33, 35–38
distillation, 85
fermentation, 73, 75, 83
ongoing process of, *ix*
personal, *viii–ix*, 8, 9
separation, 45, 55
stages of alchemical, 4–8
tools for, 11–12
True identity, separation, 6

Visualization, *viii*, 11, 114
Breath of Spirit exercise, 94, 96

Cleansing Waterfall exercise, 40
Earth-Shadow Heart Chakra
    Visualization exercise, 66
4 Element, 7 Chakra Balancing
    Visualization exercise, 107–108
Root Chakra Awakening exercise, 26
tool for transformation, 12

Water, *ix*, 10
Water Scrying, meditation
    exercise, 37–38
White Phase, 43, 114
Albedo, 43
conjunction, 43, 57–68
separation, 43, 45–55

Yeast, 7, 74

Zen, 93

Acknowledgments

No work is created in a vacuum, and I have so many people who bolster me, not only in my writing process but in life. Thanks to my family: Jim, Tanner, and Liz, who have spent years being written about. They've been there through it all, even when I starve or neglect them because I'm elbows deep in a book.

I'd also like to thank the Salty Little Beaches for being incredibly supportive and so much fun. You keep me sane and balanced so I don't become a workaholic.

To Cheryl Knight-Wilson, I thank you in every book because you were the one who told me I could be a writer, and I believed you, and you provided me with my first genuine platform to share my work.

Thanks to my friends and partners in The Vision Collective, as well as to all of my healing partners and students. You may not realize this, but you inspire me to grow every day. I am incredibly humbled to have each of you in my life.

Thank you to Jesse Aylen, my editor in the process. It's been a joy. And thank you also to Callisto Media—you have allowed me to share my truth with the world, and I am forever grateful.

About the Author

Karen Frazier writes spiritual, metaphysical, and vibrational (energy) healing books, articles, and blogs. She is a teacher, ordained metaphysical minister, intuitive energy healer, Reiki master-teacher, and psychic medium. She holds a PhD in metaphysics from the University of Sedona.

Karen writes and teaches about a number of topics related to spiritual growth, including psychic development, dream interpretation, Reiki, energy healing, meditation, feng shui, astrology, tarot, symbolism, spiritual development, crystals, sound healing, and personal growth. She also practices as an energy healer, life coach, and psychic medium.

Karen is a founding member of The Vision Collective, a Portland, Oregon–based group of spiritual teachers. She is also the host of the *Intention Is Everything* podcast as well as a writer and editor for Love-ToKnow.com. Along with writing about spiritual truths, Karen is also a food, wine, and cocktails writer. She lives near Portland, Oregon, with her husband, Jim, and her two Brussels griffons (who are the bosses of her), Monkey and Mickey.

Learn more on her website, **authorkarenfrazier.com**.

CPSIA information can be obtained
at www.ICGtesting.com
Printed in the USA
JSHW051337020321
12181JS00011B/98